PRESENTED TO
Beth Israel Library
Vineland, N. J.

Mr. and Mrs.
David Winogron

IN MEMORY OF
Their grandfather
John Fleischner

FlyAway Home

Fly Away Home

by Christine Nöstlinger

Translated from the German by Anthea Bell

Franklin Watts, Inc.   *New York*   *1975*

Maybug, maybug, fly away home!
Father to the war has gone.
Mother is living in Gunpowdertown,
Gunpowdertown is all burnt down.

Library of Congress Cataloging in Publication Data
Nöstlinger, Christine.
  Fly away home.

  SUMMARY: A young girl recalls what life was like for her family
in Vienna toward the end of World War II.

  [1. Vienna—History—Fiction. 2. World War, 1939–1945—Austria—
Fiction. 3. Austria—History—1938–1945—Fiction] I. Title.
PZ7.N672Fl3   [Fic]   75–16255
ISBN 0–531–01096–1

Foreword

The story I am going to tell here is over twenty-five years old. Clothes were different twenty-five years ago, and so were cars. Streets were different, and food was different, and we were different too, although twenty-five years ago small children in Vienna did sing the nonsense rhyme that goes:

*"Maybug, maybug, fly away home!
Father to the war has gone . . ."*

Today small Viennese children still sing:

*"Maybug, maybug, fly away home!
Father to the war has gone . . ."*

But in those days the children knew exactly what they were singing. Father really had gone to the war.

"Mother is living in Gunpowdertown . . ."

Mother really did live in Gunpowdertown, and so did we along with her.

"Gunpowdertown is all burnt down."

Though it was not the maybugs' fault if Gunpowdertown was all burnt down twenty-five years ago, any more than it is now.

The story I am going to tell is true. It happened to me. It is a tale of Gunpowdertown.

Our building—Grandmother—The radio cuckoo—
Auntie Hanni—Silver beads from the sky

I was eight years old, and I lived in Hernals, a district of Vienna. I lived in a grey, three-storeyed building. There was a yard behind the building containing dustbins, a frame for hanging carpets over to beat them, and a sawhorse. A plum tree grew at one end of the yard, by the wall where the lavatory windows were, but it never had any plums on it.

There was a cellar below the building, the best and biggest cellar in the whole block. Good cellars were important, more important than elegant living rooms or fine bedrooms, on account of the bombs. The war was on; the war had been on for a long time now, and I could not even remember a time when the war had not been on. I was used to the war, used to the bombs, of which there were a great many.

Once I saw them drop. I was at my grandmother's. She lived in the same building as we did. The last door on the ground floor led to our apartment; hers was the first door on the ground floor. Grandmother was deaf. I was sitting in her kitchen with her while she peeled potatoes, grumbling crossly about the potatoes and about the war. Before the war, said Grandmother, she'd have thrown rotten, muddy potatoes like these straight back in the greengrocer's face. She was quivering with fury at the sight of all the black marks on the potatoes. Grandmother very often quivered with fury. She was a fierce person.

The radio stood on the kitchen dresser, beside Grandmother, a small black box with a single red knob for turning it on and off and adjusting the volume. It was playing a march tune. The tune suddenly stopped, and a voice said: "Here is a warning announcement. Enemy aircraft are approaching Stein am Anger."

Afterwards there was no more military music. Grandmother

went on grumbling about the potatoes and the war, and went on to grumble about the *Blockwart*, the local Party official in charge of our block of buildings. Being deaf, she had failed to catch the radio announcement. I said, "Grandmother, the planes are coming," but not very loud. I spoke so that Grandmother would not hear me. After all, if the planes had only just got to Stein am Anger, it still wasn't certain that they would fly on to Vienna. They might turn off in another direction, and I didn't want to go down to the cellar for nothing. Grandmother always made straight for the cellar when planes reached Stein am Anger, when my mother or sister or grandfather were around to tell her they were coming.

The planes did not turn off in another direction. A squawking sound came from the radio set: "Cuck-cuck-cuck-cuck . . ."

This was a signal that the bombers were flying towards Vienna. I went to the window. There was Auntie Hanni, running down the street. Auntie Hanni was an old lady who lived three buildings away from us; the war and the bombs had made her crazy. Auntie Hanni carried a folding wooden stool under one arm and a rolled-up check rug under the other. She ran and ran, crying, "The cuckoo is calling! Listen, everyone, the cuckoo is calling!"

She would run round the block of buildings like this every time there was an air raid, round and round the block, looking for a nice safe cellar, but none of the cellars seemed to her safe enough. On and on she would run, panting and trembling and calling cuckoo, until the air raid was over. Then she would go home, set up the folding stool close to her living-room door, sit down on it, spread the check rug over her knees, and wait for the cuckoo on the radio to begin calling again.

This time, just as Auntie Hanni ran past Grandmother's kitchen window the sirens began to wail. They were placed on the roofs of the houses, and made an appalling noise. The wailing sirens meant the planes were here.

My grandmother had reached the stage of comparing the few sound potatoes with the large pile of peelings, rotten pieces, and black bits. She finished calling the greengrocer and the *Blockwart* names, and began to go on about that pig of a district leader they called the *Gauleiter* and that crazy Hitler, who had let us in for all this trouble.

"They let us in for it, they did, all the big brass, and it's poor folk like us have to take the consequences. Like putty in their hands, that's what we are," said Grandmother crossly. But when the sirens began to wail she paused. "Wasn't that the siren?" she asked.

"No, no!" I said. I *had* to say no. I couldn't, I just could not go down to the cellar with Grandmother. She was so fierce and angry. Once down in the cellar she was sure to go on complaining and calling people names: the *Blockwart*, Hitler, Goebbels, the *Gauleiter*, the greengrocer. And I didn't want Grandmother doing that; she had done far too much grumbling already, and in far too loud a voice, because she was hard of hearing, and deaf people often do talk too loud. Grandmother never said "Heil Hitler!" when she met someone, either, and right now Frau Brenner, from up on the first floor, would be sitting in the cellar. Frau Brenner always greeted people with the words "Heil Hitler!" Frau Brenner had said several times already that people like my grandmother ought to be reported to the Gestapo, because they didn't believe in the ultimate triumph of the German people, and were not helping to win the war, and were against the Führer.

I was afraid of Frau Brenner, so I kept quiet about the sirens. Grandmother put the potatoes on the gas stove, and calmed down a bit, because the gas flame was bright blue and strong, which was unusual. Of course, this was because no one else was cooking, since they were all down in the cellars.

There was no one in sight on the street, only Auntie Hanni running along Kalvarienberggasse, in the distance. I could just catch her voice as she cried, "The cuckoo is calling! The cuckoo is calling!"

I looked up at the sky. It was forget-me-not blue. And then I saw the bombers. There were a lot of them, flying in formation with one plane at the head, then two more, three behind those two, and a great many others following. The planes were beautiful, shining in the sun. Then they dropped their bombs. This was something I had never seen before, because usually I was down in the cellar. It was very different down there. People sat waiting, ducking their heads when a rushing sound came through the air; then the explosion would come, and after that it was quiet again, and someone would say, "That was close!" Then everyone would straighten up again, feeling glad the bombs had fallen somewhere else, and their own building was still standing and they were still alive.

This time, however, I could see the bombs. So many of them were dropped from the planes one · by one, and they were dropped so fast, that they looked like strings of shining, silvery beads hanging from each aircraft. Then the strings of beads broke and the bombs came whizzing down. They were very loud, louder than anything I had ever heard before, so loud that even Grandmother could hear them. Grandmother seized me and tried to drag me away from the window. "Down to the cellar, quick!" she shouted. "Run!"

I couldn't run. I couldn't even move. I clung to the window sill. Grandmother pulled me away from the window and dragged me through the kitchen, along the passage, down to the cellar door. The bombs were still falling, and the noise was even louder than before. It drummed against my head, rushed in my ears, made my nose prickle and my throat tighten. Grandmother pushed me down the cellar steps, stumbling down after me and falling on top of me. We landed at the bottom of the worn steps together, and the cellar door slammed shut behind us.

We sat on the bottom step. The cellar light had gone out, and it was dark. I leaned against Grandmother. Grandmother was trembling and crying. There were rushing, crashing noises overhead. The cellar door swung open and shut, open and shut.

Suddenly everything was quiet. Grandmother stopped sobbing and trembling. My head was resting on her plump, soft bosom, and she was stroking me. "They're going away," she murmured. "Going away again!"

The all-clear siren sounded. The all-clear was a pleasant, soft, long, drawn-out note. There was a light at the end of the passage leading to the cellar; it was a big torch belonging to the warden of our building. I heard his voice. "Everyone keep calm. I'm going up to have a look. Don't panic, please."

Grandmother and I climbed the cellar steps along with the warden. Our building was undamaged, except for a few window panes broken by the tremendous pressure caused by the exploding bombs. We went out into the street. People were emerging from other doors as well.

At one end of the street, at the junction with Kalvarienberggasse, we saw a big cloud of dust, and by the junction with the Gürtel a big building and the smaller building that used to stand beside it were gone.

Auntie Hanni's husband came up to us. "Have you seen Hanni anywhere?" he asked. His face looked very grey and tired. "I've been looking for her all over the place."

No, we had not seen Auntie Hanni. We never saw Auntie Hanni again; she was lying in Kalvarienberggasse, buried under a heap of rubble. Her husband dug her out. But for the folding stool under one arm and the check rug under the other, he would not have known her, because her head was blown off.

But we did not know that at the time.

"Why don't you go down to the Pezzlpark bunker?" suggested the warden. "Have a look there. She might have gone into that bunker."

Auntie Hanni's husband shook his head. "She won't be there! She's never been in that bunker . . . she won't go into any bunker."

Auntie Hanni's husband went away. My grandmother, watching him go, began to tremble again. Suddenly she shouted, "To hell with Hitler! Heil Hitler! To hell with Hitler!"

"Please, please!" said the warden. "Keep quiet, for heaven's sake! It's dangerous to talk that way!"

But Grandmother would not keep quiet. She went on and on shouting, like a gramophone record with the needle stuck in a groove, "To hell with Hitler! Heil Hitler! To hell with Hitler! Heil Hitler! To hell with Hitler!"

The warden got Grandmother into the building, with my help; he pulled and I pushed, pummelling desperately at Grandmother's behind.

Gradually Grandmother calmed down. She leaned against the passage wall, muttering, "My potatoes! My potatoes—they're still on the stove! They'll be burnt to a cinder!"

Grandmother hurried into her kitchen, with me after her, but her potatoes were not burnt. The gas had gone out; a bomb must have fallen on the main somewhere.

5

Grandfather—Going out with the bag—
The woman in the coffeehouse—
The black marketeer—Lemon candy

Grandfather lived in Grandmother's apartment too. I was
very fond of Grandfather. He was tall and thin, with a white
moustache, violet-blue eyes, a middle parting in his hair, and hair
growing out of his ears. When Grandmother was not around he
could tell stories and be very funny. But Grandfather was frightened of Grandmother; he was frightened of a lot of things. He
was frightened of going to the Tax Office, he was frightened if a
policeman looked at him, and he was frightened when he tried to
get the English broadcasts on the radio—not that he ever succeeded. But worst of all he was frightened of Grandmother. I
always thought Grandfather must have married Grandmother
because he was frightened of her. She probably gave him one of
her fierce looks and said, "Lepold, you are going to marry me!"
    And no doubt Grandfather said, "Yes, Juli, all right, Juli!"
out of sheer fright.
    However, perhaps it had not been like that at all, and
Grandfather had once loved Grandmother very much and she
had loved him back. But as far as I could tell nothing of the sort
was noticeable. Grandmother never spoke a kind word to Grandfather. It was always: "Lepold, time to be off! Lepold, fetch the
coal up from the cellar! Lepold, close the window! Lepold, turn
the light off! Lepold, give me the newspaper! Lepold, listen to
me! Lepold, give me some money!"
    Grandfather always answered, "Yes, Juli, all right, Juli!"
    His real name was Leopold, and Grandmother's was Julia.
    Grandfather had a funny kind of job; he sold spare parts for
clocks—all the little wheels and screws and springs you find
inside the clockwork. However, he did not have a shop with a

window and a sign above it. He kept all his spare parts in two boxes in the little closet behind Grandmother's kitchen. Sometimes a watchmaker would come and see him to buy a spring or a wheel or a little bag of screws, but usually Grandfather took his stock-in-trade round to the watchmakers' shops. Grandmother called this "going out with the bag."

Every weekday, after breakfast, Grandfather packed his big black bag and set off, and when he came home in the evening, he would take off his black lace-up shoes and his black socks, rub his long, thin toes, and murmur, "Dear me, dear me, what a long way I've walked today! Hardly sold a thing, either. There are only doddery, short-sighted old watchmakers left these days. All the others are in the army!"

Then Grandfather would fetch the white enamel basin from the kitchen, fill it with water, put it on the floor under the table, roll up the legs of his striped trousers, sit down at the table and put his feet in the basin of water, shivering because it was cold. Grandmother would not let him have any warm water to bathe his feet. She didn't think much of footbaths in any case.

Then Grandmother got supper: potatoes with dill on Monday, baked potatoes on Tuesday, potato pancakes with turnips on Wednesday, potato purée on Thursday, potato goulash on Friday and potato cakes on Saturday. This weekly menu of potato dishes never varied. Grandmother only once went wrong, when she made potato cakes on a Tuesday, and on that occasion she was all excited because she had won thirty marks in the lottery. Directly afterwards she got very angry because she found that there was nothing she could buy with her thirty marks. Grandmother ran back to the lottery ticket office and flung her thirty marks down on the table in front of the woman there, shouting, "Here you are! You can put that silly bit of paper in your pipe and smoke it! *I* can't get anything for it. So much for your stupid money! Why don't you give meat coupons for prizes instead—at least they'd be worth something!"

I stood in the ticket office doorway, feeling horribly embarrassed because of Grandmother.

Grandfather grumbled a great deal about his poor feet, and the way he had walked round with his bag and sold nothing. Grandmother did not feel sorry for him—Grandmother never felt sorry for anyone—but she believed him. As it happened, Grand-

7

father was deceiving her; he did not really do much walking about at all, as I very well knew, because sometimes, when there was no school, Grandfather would take me with him.

I enjoyed going out with Grandfather and his bag. First we would go to the coffeehouse. Grandfather knew a woman who ran a coffeehouse, a small coffeehouse with red plush upholstery, and she was fond of Grandfather. She gave him real coffee, and often there was nut strudel, with raisins in it too. There was a fat old dog in the coffeehouse. He had lost all his teeth and was lame in one leg.

The lady in the coffeehouse had a husband who must have been every bit as fierce as Grandmother. The coffeehouse lady often told us about her husband, and afterwards she would always add, "It's a dreadful thing to say, but I wouldn't mind if the war went on for ever. At least I get a bit of peace from *him!*" For the owner of the coffeehouse was in Russia with the army.

After going to the coffeehouse, Grandfather and I would call on a watchmaker, and I was allowed to choose which one. Little Herr Mauritz was my favourite. He was barely a metre tall, and he used to stand on some wooden steps so that he could see over the top of his counter.

I also liked visiting the man who repaired antique clocks. There was a sign above his shop saying "The Clock Studio," and it was full of all kinds of clocks: musical clocks, grandfather clocks, pendulum clocks. Somewhere in the place there was always a tinkling little tune playing, or a pendulum clock striking the wrong hour. In fact, the man who repaired these old clocks did not need any of Grandfather's spare parts. He had given up repairing clocks a long time ago and become a black marketeer instead. This was a dangerous profession; if the police caught you at it, you were arrested and taken off to a concentration camp. The antique clock man was always very kind to me. When Grandfather and I went into his shop the first thing he always said was, "This is an honour, a great honour, Herr Göth!" (Besides Leopold, my grandfather's name was Göth.) Then he would say, "And how is our pretty little poppet today?"

By pretty little poppet he meant me. He would take me into his dark back room, open a cupboard and bring out a box full of soft, sticky lemon candy. With some difficulty, I would fish out a piece of the lemony mush, trying not to be too greedy. Sometimes

I got a really big lump, so big I could hardly suck it because my mouth was so full.

Each time I left the shop with Grandfather, I told myself, "I won't suck it all this time. I'll leave a bit for Schurli Berger today."

Schurli Berger lived in the same building as us, on the second floor, and he was my best friend. Even so, I never did manage to bring him home a piece of lemon candy.

My mother could not stand the man who owned the Clock Studio. The reason for this was that once my mother came by a lot of money, a legacy from an old aunt who died. In the evening, when the shops were closed, my mother went to see the antique clock man. She gave him all the money, and in return he got her three kilos of bacon and four kilos of sugar. My mother had expected to get half a pig, at least, for all that money, but the antique clock man just laughed at her and said that money was worth nothing in times like these. Half a pig! She'd need to give a piano, or five winter coats, for half a pig, he said. We didn't own five winter coats, but we did have a piano. My sister and I had to practise on it every day, and once a week we went to see a lady called Frau Kriegelstein and play her what we had been practising. Frau Kriegelstein would sit on a chair beside us, counting, "One, two, three, one two three, one, two, three." Then she would heave a deep sigh. She must have thought us very unmusical.

We would have been delighted to swap the piano for half a pig—even for three eggs. But my mother would not hear of such a thing, and was furious when we suggested it, as furious as even Grandmother could be. My mother had saved for four years to buy that piano, and now it made her furious to think of having saved for four years to buy three eggs or half a pig. She could not see any sense in it.

My father in hospital—The Brenners' dog—
The doll's house—Brick dust—
The crack in the ceiling

Spring came very early in the year 1945, which was lucky, because we had no wood or coal left for fires. Even better, my father came back from the front in March.

My father was in a military hospital in Vienna now. Before that he had been in hospital in Germany, and before that again he had been in hospital in Poland, and before the Polish hospital he had been in a railway train in Russia, a train without an engine stuck somewhere on the tracks, my father and thirty other soldiers lying in a flat car with Russian planes flying low overhead. My father's legs were riddled with shot, and there were shell splinters all over his body. However, he could manage to limp about, though with difficulty, and every morning he got a pass at the hospital and was allowed to come home to us and stay till evening.

It was neither chance nor luck that my father was in hospital in Vienna; my uncle, my mother's brother, had wangled it. He was a high-up SS man at the Führer's headquarters in Berlin. Nor was the fact that my father got a pass every day chance either. Among Grandfather's stock of spare parts, right at the very bottom of the closet, there were still some timepieces: watches, alarm clocks, a kitchen clock. Grandfather had hoarded them up like treasure, and now they were finding their way to the non-commissioned officer at the hospital. In return, the NCO wrote out passes for my father.

The Russians were not far from Vienna now, though no one knew exactly where they were. School was closed almost every other day, because of overnight bombing raids—not that it made much difference, for we could hardly have learned much in any case. We had pupils from two other primary schools in our school now, because their own buildings had been bombed.

Frau Brenner still said "Heil Hitler!" when she met people, and Frau Sula, who came to clean Frau Brenner's windows once a week, said that Frau Brenner had stored up a whole lot of poison. When the Russians came, Frau Brenner was going to poison herself, and Herr Brenner, and Hedi Brenner, and the Brenners' dog. I felt sorry for the Brenners' dog.

Then a day came when the air-raid sirens on the rooftops wailed at five o'clock in the morning. They wailed again at seven, and at eight. By midday there was only one siren still capable of wailing; the rest were lying on the heaps of rubble, among tiles and bits of wall and broken doors and windows and fallen chimneys. My father said we were lucky all the same: the Americans were not dropping incendiary bombs, the kind that started fires.

We had been down in the cellar for ten hours, and we were hungry, but no one dared leave the building to fetch food. No one dared leave the cellar. There was no lavatory there, and we had to crouch down in a corner. My friend Schurli Berger chanted a rude rhyme about the combat troops in Stein am Anger. Frau Brenner was annoyed, and started babbling as usual about "Suppose the Führer could hear you!" Frau Berger, Schurli's mother, looked Frau Brenner up and down and said deliberately, "You and your Führer! Your Führer can lick my arse, that's all *I've* got to say!"

The rest of us sheltering in the cellar nodded approvingly.

When the bomb hit our building, it made no more noise than when the building next door had gone an hour earlier, and there was not much more of a tremor either. But the whole cellar was filled with brick dust, and plaster fell off the walls. So did a few bricks. One of them fell on Herr Benedikt's head. Herr Benedikt was Schurli Berger's uncle. Herr Benedikt was very frightened, and tried to get out of the cellar, striking out in a panic and pushing aside anyone who was in his way. He hit me in the stomach. It hurt.

The woman from next door cried, "We're buried! Buried alive! We'll never get out!"

She was wrong; we were not buried. The cellar door had been torn off its hinges and was lying on the cellar steps, with a ladder and the caretaker's wife's birdcage (minus the bird) and a lot of bricks and rubble on top of it. But it was quite easy to clear all this away and get out.

Our building resembled a rather shabby doll's house. Half of it had collapsed, and the other half stood open to the air, looking helpless and very forlorn with its rooms chopped in two. The staircase had gone as well.

Frau Benedikt was unable to grasp the fact that though her wardrobe was still leaning against the pink wall of her bedroom on the second floor, no one would go and get her thick winter coat out of it. I clambered about on the heaps of rubble, which I was not really supposed to do, in case they collapsed, but no one had time to keep an eye on me. I found a number of familiar objects among the rubble. There was Herr Benedikt's pendulum clock, one of our green kitchen curtains, our neighbour's big brown bottle of mouthwash, and part of Frau Brenner's red velvet sofa. I also found the wheel of a doll's pram, but I could not be sure if it was mine or not. And I came upon a big white box containing twelve bright, gleaming Christmas tree ornaments, packed in cotton. Not one of them was broken.

The pile of ruins on which I was sitting was about five metres high. The building used to be fourteen metres high. I thought of going to look for a stick five metres long. My bed ought to be about five metres below me. Or was I sitting on top of the kitchen? But I was thirsty, because of the brick dust; brick dust sticks to your lips and tongue and gets into your throat. So I clambered down from the rubble.

Grandmother's apartment was in the half of the building which was still standing, and we went inside. Half the kitchen was gone, but the room beyond it was all right. There was a great crack right across the ceiling, though, and my sister was afraid of this crack and did not want to go into the room. Grandfather stayed with her, in the half-kitchen, and I went into the room with Grandmother. Grandmother picked up pieces of broken flowerpot, cleared jagged glass out of the window frames, wiped brick dust off the furniture. I crouched on the double bed. It was dusty. I looked at the crack in the ceiling.

My mother went off to the ration card distribution centre for a bomb permit. This was important; you could exchange a bomb permit for a woollen blanket and something new to wear—even, it was said, a pair of leather-soled shoes—but only if you could prove you had lost everything.

My father limped off to the hospital, since he was supposed to be back at five. His limp was worse than usual, because several pieces of brick had fallen on his infected legs as he helped clear away the rubble. Grandmother put her head out of the empty window frame to watch my father go, muttering (and being deaf, she muttered very loud), "Poor boy, poor boy . . ." Then she began to shout, "The brutes! The swine! The scoundrels! What have you done to my boy, you scoundrels?"

Grandfather came out of the half-kitchen and pulled Grandmother away from the window. "Juli, Juli!" he said. "Juli, stop it, the *Blockwart* is going round the block!"

Grandmother threw herself across the table, drumming on the tabletop with her fists, her feet flailing in the air, and went on shouting, "Swine! Scoundrels!"

Grandfather tried to put his hand over her mouth, but Grandmother bit it. Grandfather yelled in pain. Then Grandmother stopped shouting and beating her fists on the table and kicking her legs in the air. She just lay where she was, flat across the table, crying. Grandfather took her glasses off her nose, found his handkerchief in his trouser pocket and gave it to her.

My mother came back from the ration card centre with the bomb permits, and two blankets; there were no shoes or clothes left. I was still staring at the crack in the ceiling. It was beginning to get dark. I could not see the crack properly any more, but I knew I had to keep watching it. "It's too dark!" I cried. "Turn the light on! If you don't the crack will get bigger and bigger and everything will fall on our heads."

My mother said the electric light was gone, and so were the oil lamps, and we had no candles. But Grandmother did find a candle end, and lit it. The flame flickered wildly, because there was no glass in the windows, and the wind was coming into the room. Grandmother climbed onto the table, holding the flickering candle end, and held it up to the crack in the ceiling. The crack had not got any bigger. I fell asleep.

Frau von Braun—Frau von Braun's villa—An offer

Next morning Frau von Braun came to see us. I woke up in Grandmother's double bed to find my sister lying beside me, still asleep. She was snorting in her sleep, and her forehead and nose were all dusty.

There was Frau von Braun with her hooked, red nose, wearing her plush coat, standing in Grandmother's room, and Grandfather was asking if her place had been bombed too.

Frau von Braun shook her head in horror, as if to say: My place, indeed! Such things do not happen to the Frau von Brauns of this world!

Frau von Braun sat down on the double bed, quite close to me, and I drew away from her. She tapped the floor with her silver-topped walking stick, once or twice, and the brick dust swirled up. Grandmother fetched a duster to wipe it away.

"I have a summer villa out at Neuwaldegg," Frau von Braun informed us. Neuwaldegg is a residential suburb of Vienna. She hardly needed to tell us about her villa there; everyone in the district knew about it. We all knew Frau von Braun too. She was as old as the hills, and rich, and aristocratic. She was also a Nazi.

The Russians were not far from Vienna now, and the Americans kept dropping bombs, and being a Nazi was not such a good thing these days. Old Frau von Braun had come to the conclusion that her Führer and the Fatherland no longer needed her presence here in Vienna, and she was going off to her farm in the Tyrol. It would be nice and peaceful there, with no Russians and no bombs.

However, Frau von Braun was worried about her summer villa in Neuwaldegg. One did not like to leave such a large and beautiful house empty, Frau von Braun explained, especially in times like these, when there was so much riffraff in Vienna! So

Frau von Braun was in urgent need of someone to look after her villa for her while she was in the Tyrol, and she was suggesting that we should go and take care of it.

My grandmother could not make out what Frau von Braun said. "What does she want? What's she saying?" Grandmother asked.

Grandfather shouted Frau von Braun's proposition into Grandmother's ear. Grandmother waved a dismissive hand, and looked up at the crack in the ceiling. "That'll hold a long time yet!" she said. "It'll see Hitler's thousand-year Reich out, anyway."

My grandfather sighed. Obviously he would have liked to go to Neuwaldegg himself, but Grandmother gave him one of her fierce looks, and Grandfather decided that he too preferred to stay in the room with the crack in the ceiling. "I'm sorry, ma'am," he told Frau von Braun. "Juli doesn't want to. We can't."

However, my mother had nowhere at all left to live now, not even a room with a crack in the ceiling, and she accepted Frau von Braun's offer. She even thanked Frau von Braun profusely.

Frau von Braun instructed us not to touch the furniture in the villa, to leave the carpets rolled up, to clean the shutters, to water the flower beds, not to scratch the parquet flooring, and to keep the front door and the garden gate locked at all times. My mother promised to do all these things, and it made me very angry to see her standing so meekly in front of this old woman with the hooked red nose, saying, "Yes, Frau von Braun . . . Of course, Frau von Braun . . . Why, naturally, Frau von Braun!"

Then Frau von Braun gave my mother the keys to the villa, told her which key opened the big gate and which key opened the little one, said "Heil Hitler!," tapped the floor once or twice more with her silver-topped stick, and then clambered off over the bricks, broken lavatory pans and window frames. There was a Wehrmacht car waiting for her in the street.

The army car drove off. Grandmother watched it go, but she did not shout anything out of the window after it; she had done more than her share of shouting over the last few days. She felt tired.

The Als—A waste of bombs—Pickled breasts— A forged pass

We set off that afternoon, my mother, my sister and myself, to walk to Neuwaldegg. The trams had been off the streets for weeks now, and we followed the tramlines. I counted the bomb craters in the street. There were some particularly impressive ones in the Alszeile, along which we were walking now. The Als flows through an underground tunnel here, and the bombs had gone right through the street above it.

I stood at the edge of one bomb crater with my sister, while my mother held our shoulders, staring down into the black water. All the local drains run into the Als, and it stank to high heaven.

We saw something swimming past. My mother said it was a rat. Then a *Blockwart* wearing a swastika armband came along, and told us it was dangerous to stand too close to bomb craters, and we must move on. My mother called after the man, "Is there anything that's *not* dangerous these days, Herr Blockwart?"

He did not reply, or even turn round.

Our shoes had wooden soles; leather-soled shoes had been impossible to get for a long time. Walking in shoes with wooden soles is difficult. Your feet burn and sting, and you get blisters. When we reached the tramline terminus we sat down on a bench. I took my shoes off and put my hot feet on the cool ground; that felt nice. There was a nail in my sister's shoe somewhere which hurt her, and my mother tried to get it out.

It was quiet and peaceful here at the tramline terminus. There were no factories and no big apartment blocks in this district, and no bomb ruins either, only pretty villas in big gardens. Not a single villa had been damaged. I asked, "Why don't the Americans drop bombs on Neuwaldegg?"

"It would be a waste of bombs," said my mother. "They'd only kill about four people with one bomb."

"And suppose it fell in the garden," my sister told me, "it might only kill a pear tree or something, and bombs are too expensive to be wasted like that, you see."

I saw. My sister was older than me and knew about things like that. I was glad to be in a part of Vienna which was too expensive for bombs.

I was just putting my wooden shoes on again when I saw a man limping along the road. The man wore a grey uniform, and he looked like my father. "Here comes Daddy!" I cried.

My mother was tired, leaning back on the bench, eyes closed. She did not open them. "Daddy's in the hospital," she said. "He can't come today. They're taking some of the shell splinters out of his left leg today. Perhaps he'll come and see us tomorrow, or the day after."

The man in the grey uniform was very close now, and it *was* my father. He sat down on the bench beside us, put his crutch between his knees, rested his head on top of it, and said, "Well, that's the end of the war for me!"

We stared at my father. He just smiled. "The whole place was upside down this morning," he went on. "Orders had come for the whole hospital to be evacuated to Germany, because the Russians are getting so close. Everyone had to go, even men who'd just come off the operating table."

"But what about you?" asked my mother. "Don't you have to go too? Why not?"

"I ran for it," said my father. "From the train. The whistle had already sounded, and in all the confusion no one noticed. Scuttling around like chickens, they were, scared to death!"

I sat quite still, trying not to be afraid. But I was not a fool, and I knew very well that a soldier is still a soldier, however sick or wounded or full of shell splinters he may be. He is not free to do as he likes, he must obey orders. And a soldier who is sitting on a park bench in Neuwaldegg instead of in the train for Germany is a deserter, and deserters get shot. These days they were getting shot without any trial or legal proceedings at all—simply shot.

"Let's go on," said my mother, who was suddenly in a great hurry. We stood up. The nail in my sister's shoe was still hurting her, and I had a big, watery blister on the sole of my foot. I felt it burst.

"Not far now," said my sister. I took her hand.

We hardly met a soul, though sometimes we glimpsed some-one behind a garden fence. Shutters were down over the windows of most of the villas.

"They've all gone off to the West," said my mother. "They're afraid of the Russians."

"The Russians cut off women's breasts, and shoot children, and loot houses, and set fire to everything, and burn it all down," said my sister.

"Who told you all that nonsense?" said my father.

My sister shrugged her shoulders. "Well, that's what everybody says at school. The gym mistress says so, and the other children, and Frau Brenner. They say so at the *Bund Deutscher Mädchen* too." The *Bund Deutscher Mädchen* was the Nazi youth organisation for girls.

"Schurli Berger told me," I said. "And his uncle told him about the Russians cutting up some women into little bits—and they put the bits in tubs of brine and pickle them."

"What for?" asked my sister. But I had no more idea than she did *why* the Russians were pickling people.

At the junction of Atariastrasse and Neuwaldegger Strasse we came to a Wehrmacht open car with two soldiers on patrol leaning on the hood. They were very young, thin soldiers.

"What now?" asked my mother softly.

"Keep going—just keep going!" said my father.

My sister was still holding my hand. Her fingers were hot and damp, and she held my hand very tight. The closer we came to the soldiers, the tighter she clung.

We were level with the Wehrmacht car now, and one of the soldiers barred our way and asked my father for his papers. My father took his paybook out of his coat pocket, and the soldiers examined it. Then my father handed them a piece of paper. The soldiers looked long and hard at this piece of paper, nodded, gave it back to my father, saluted and stepped aside.

We went on. Three houses to go. We reached the garden gate of Number 58, and my mother took the bunch of keys Frau von Braun had given her out of her bag. She tried to unlock the garden gate, but the key was trembling in her hand. My father took it and unlocked the gate.

A small door opened in the big, ornamental iron gate. Before stepping into the garden, I looked back down the street. The two young, thin soldiers were leaning against the Wehrmacht car again, and one of them was just lighting a cigarette.

"What made the patrol let you through?" asked my mother. We were walking up a broad gravel path towards the big villa, which was bright yellow stucco outside.

My father took the paper he had shown the soldiers out of his pocket. "My pass," he said, grinning. "I'll make myself out another one tomorrow!" He tapped the inside breast pocket of his uniform jacket. "I've got all I need in here," he said. "Enough to equip an office! Pass forms, rubber stamps, the lot!"

"Where did you get it?" asked my mother.

"Well, it wasn't exactly a present . . . it just happened to be lying around the office back at the hospital, and I prudently helped myself."

My mother sighed. "Do you think you'll get away with it?"

My father did not answer her.

"If the Russians don't come soon, the Germans will get you!" said my mother.

"When are the Russians coming?" asked my sister.

My mother shrugged her shoulders.

"The Russians are coming soon," said my father. "Very soon."

The salon—The uncles—The garden gnomes— The summerhouses—Venus von Braun

Frau von Braun's villa was very large and very yellow. The shutters were brown, and the roof was grey. There was a round terrace and a square terrace, a long, narrow balcony and a short, wide balcony. There were three bay windows, a little turret and a big turret, and two flagstaffs.

I had never seen such a house in my life before. The biggest place I knew was Margit Koch's apartment, where they had a living room, a bedroom, a kitchen, a dining room, and a nursery. But there were other, and extraordinary, kinds of rooms in Frau von Braun's house. There was a huge great room just for books, with books all round the walls—books with thick, dark brown leather bindings, and gold lettering on their backs.

Another room had five windows, and my mother said it was called a "salon," which is a French word for a drawing room. The word reminded me of Herr Hampersek the tailor, who had a sign over his door saying "Otto Hampersek: Tailoring Saloon." Herr Tonio Pellegrini used to have a similar sign saying "Italian Ice Cream Saloon," but he had had to close his ice cream saloon a long time ago. However, Frau von Braun's salon was not like either of these saloons; it was no good for anything, just full of armchairs shrouded in shapeless grey linen covers. There was even a grey linen cover over a huge object hanging from the ceiling. Probably there was a glittering glass chandelier inside. The linen covers were to keep the dust off, and we were told not to remove them. This was not our own house, said my mother.

And there were a great many other rooms, rooms which were not living rooms, or bedrooms, or dining rooms, and certainly not nurseries. Rooms on the ground floor, on the first floor, up in the attic. And there were wooden monsters swathed in grey linen everywhere, and rolled-up carpets in the corners. It felt weird walking through the rooms as dusk fell in the evening.

There were big glass folding doors between the various rooms. If my sister stood in the middle of one room and stamped on the parquet floor as hard as she could, the glass doors would fly open all by themselves.

We liked the room we called the Uncles' Room, which was really a music room, we were told. The only piece of furniture in it was a huge piano with two piano stools. The walls were covered with oil paintings. Not just side by side, but on top of each other and under each other as well, and with more paintings leaning up in the corners of the room. Each picture was the portrait of a man. My sister and I used to play a game called Guess the Uncle in the Uncles' Room. I would sit on one of the piano stools, turn round and unobtrusively pick out one particular portrait. My sister would sit on the other piano stool and try to guess which uncle I was thinking of.

"Has he got bright blue pop-eyes?" she asked.

I nodded.

"Has he got great big sticking-out ears?" she asked.

I nodded.

"Has he got a beard?" she asked.

I nodded again.

"Does it divide into two little points?"

I shook my head.

When at last she asked, "Is it the left-hand uncle in the top row of the right-hand wall by the window?" I would bring down all ten fingers on the piano keys so loud that the uncles on the walls swayed and shook.

Guess the Uncle was not an easy game, as all the uncles looked very much alike. They all had bright blue pop-eyes, and beards, and receding hair, and their ears all stuck out.

Frau von Braun's garden was as remarkable as her house. We found trees and shrubs we had never seen before. There was one tree that looked like a fir tree but couldn't be, because it had tiny bright yellow flowers. A statue of a naked woman with no arms or nose stood in a large flower bed.

"Her arms are missing on purpose," my mother told us, "but her nose has got broken. She did have a nose once."

There was a meadow behind the house with a shallow little stream flowing through it. My mother said it was the Als, but I did not believe her. After all, I'd seen the Als myself, through the bomb craters in the Alszeile. The Als was deep and black and smelly, and there had been a rat swimming in it.

There were two summerhouses in the garden too, a little one and a big one. They were locked, and we did not have the keys, but that didn't stop me from having a standing quarrel with my sister about them, she claiming that the big summerhouse ought to be hers because she was older than me.

We also quarrelled over the garden gnomes. Frau von Braun had thirteen of them, dotted about the various flower beds. My sister carted them off to the meadow behind the house, where we played Families with them. My sister was the father of the family, I was the mother, and the garden gnomes were our children. But we did not want thirteen children, only three, and we could never agree as to which of the garden gnomes made the best children. The one with the wheelbarrow, or the one holding the basket of flowers, or the one with the basket on his back, or the one with the lantern, or the one with the spade? The only point on which we did agree was that the garden gnome carrying a whetstone was out of the running. A child who was always sharpening knives would be a nuisance.

My father stayed indoors all the time. We could not risk having him seen. He spent most of his time lying on the floor in the room full of books. He had unrolled the carpet in this room, despite Frau von Braun's instructions, and he was reading the thick old books. Sometimes he would read aloud a passage to me, if it caught his fancy, and though I did not understand a word I nodded enthusiastically. He made us little paper boats too, using pages torn from a book he had found in Frau von Braun's desk. There was a big black swastika on the cover of this book. Inside, it contained the Führer's speeches.

Sometimes we climbed up to the attic with my father, climbed out of one of the attic windows onto the roof, and lay there in the sun. Up there, no one could see my father, since our house was much taller than its neighbours.

I told my father about all the things I had found in the house and garden: the stone woman with no arms or nose, the fir tree with bright yellow flowers, the tiny stream that my mother said was the Als. When my father said so too, I believed him. He christened the stone woman "Venus von Braun," and invented pretty names for the strange trees. We called one of them an Indonesian Cherry, and another one a Quivering Milliwillow.

My mother was out a good deal; it was half an hour's walk to the dairy, it took her three-quarters of an hour to get to the butcher's, and she had to wait in line for an hour at the baker's. When she came back, she would have quarter of a litre of milk, a hundred grams of grey, glutinous sausage, and half a loaf of crumbly, yellowish-grey bread. It was impossible to slice the bread; we had to tear pieces off it. The sausage had a strong smell and tasted of flour and rancid fat. The milk was thin and pale blue.

Once or twice my mother walked right into Vienna and went all over the city with our bomb permit, looking for a shop which still had underwear and shoes in stock, but she could not find one.

We did desperately need some clothes. We had found some towels and teacloths and bedding in the house, but nothing in the way of shirts or underclothes. No toothbrushes or soap either, let alone dresses or suits or shoes. Our most pressing need was a jacket and shirt and pair of trousers for my father, who could hardly confront the Russians when they arrived wearing the uniform of a German soldier.

My mother went into the city on foot once again to visit all our family friends and relatives—those who had not been bombed out. She returned with a big parcel of clothes. She even had some sheets—and five pairs of trousers for my father.

"Men's trousers . . ." said my mother. "Oh, I could have taken another dozen pairs of trousers!"

She told us how sad and dreadful it had been: how Aunt Hermi had taken all Uncle Toni's trousers and jackets out of the wardrobe, sobbing, "Take them, do. He won't be needing them any more! A corpse doesn't need an Esterhazy suit!"

However, my mother did not take Uncle Toni's trousers, because Uncle Toni had been short and stout, and his trousers would never have fit my father. Aunt Hermi's next-door neighbour's husband, who was tall and thin, had been killed too. My mother got trousers for my father from Aunt Hermi's neighbour.

She had a pair of beautiful leather shoes for me, red with white laces. Unfortunately, they were too small, but my father cut holes in their toes so that I could stick my big toe through, and then they fit all right. There was a dress for me too, though it was too long and too baggy. It also had an unpleasant rose pattern, and I refused to put it on, but it was no use; they put the horrid dress on me by force, and my sister roared with laughter and said, "You look like a flowered quilt!"

Barter—Going round the fence—
The Forestry Commissioner—The Angel—
Herr Wawra—Herr Goldmann

Twice a week Grandfather came to see us. The journey took him three hours; he was not such a fast walker as he used to be. He always brought something with him, something he had dug out of the piles of rubble. He salvaged some very strange things: a baby's bath, two dishes with red and white spots, a ladle, a woollen shawl, a razor, a pair of scissors, a bottle of scent, an old skirt, a pullover full of holes made by bomb splinters. My mother unravelled the shawl and the tattered pullover; she wanted to knit us cardigans with the wool, but she had no knitting needles. She searched the whole house for knitting needles. "Bother these people!" she said crossly. "They have just about everything in this place—chandeliers, oil paintings, china dogs, the lot! But not a single knitting needle!"

She picked up the baby's bath and went out. An hour later she came back in triumph with some knitting needles. Somewhere or other she had traded the bath for them.

Planes flew over our house every day, but we were not afraid of them. They were making for the city; they did not drop their bombs on us.

Every morning I made my round of the fence, beginning at the big garden gate. The fence between the garden and the road was tall here, and made of stout, black iron railings. They looked like spears interwoven with iron flowers and iron curls and iron scrolls. The iron spears were set in a knee-high red brick wall, and there were three strands of rusty barbed wire up at the top, wound round the speartips. It was a strong fence. There was a thick box hedge on the garden side. I would push my way through this hedge and then climb the iron curls and scrolls of the fence to look over the top. On the other side of the road stood an empty house whose owners had run away to the West. I made up my mind to explore this house sometime. A cellar window left half-opened was clearly visible from the top of our fence, and I was going to climb in that way. I had it all planned. I only had to wait until the old Forestry Commissioner who lived in the villa next door took his two bulldogs for their walk.

On this particular day, then, I surveyed the situation from up among the speartips. The cellar window was still half-opened, all right. The Commissioner was sitting out on his terrace having breakfast—a boiled egg. The dogs were lying beside him. I waited a moment in case the Commissioner's wife was going to come out and suggest going for a walk. She did not come out. The bulldogs yawned.

I travelled along the iron spears, hand over hand, but cautiously, so as not to scratch myself on the barbed wire. I was keeping a careful lookout for cats, soldiers, Wehrmacht cars—and the first Russian.

When I came to the end of the fence of spears I clambered down, pushed my way back through the box hedge, and went on to the fence of the garden next door. This was an ordinary wire fence. The Angel was waiting for me. The Angel was a little girl of about my own size, but otherwise quite different. She had fair curly hair, and a silk hair ribbon. It was a different ribbon every day, and the Angel wore a different dress every day as well. Her dresses were made of velvet, or pretty flower-sprigged material, or they had cross-stitch embroidery on them. I called her "the Angel" because her surname was Engel, the German word for "angel"; her full name was Susanna Maria Engel.

First I took a look at the Angel, noted that today's dress was made of checked silk, and so was her hair ribbon. Then I made a face and went "Yaaaah!" putting my tongue right out at her. Then I strolled slowly along by the wire fence. The Angel walked along beside me on the other side of the fence. Usually she was pushing a red doll's pram containing a black cat dressed up in doll's clothes and a baby's bonnet. The cat did not like it. It mewed and squirmed and tried to jump out of the pram, but the

Angel pushed it back down again, covering it up with a pink silk quilt and lisping, "No, no, darling! Be a good baby! Go to bed-die-bye!"

"I've got a much better doll's pram than that at home!" I said.

The Angel raised her eyebrows and smiled. "Where is it, then? Let's have a look at your doll's pram!"

"I'm not showing it to *you!*" I said.

"You haven't really got one at all!"

"Oh, yes, I have!" I shouted.

"Oh, no, you haven't! You've got nothing! Nothing! Nothing at all!"

The Angel made this statement very firmly and deliberately, pushing the poor cat down in the pram again.

"Let that cat go, you silly thing!" I said.

"It's my cat! It's nothing to do with you," said the Angel, adding, "And I've got two guinea pigs in the kitchen, and a canary and a white mouse, so there! And my uncle has four dogs!"

"So have I!" I shouted.

The Angel shook her head. By now we had reached the end of the fence, so I said "Yaaaah!" again and turned my back on her.

"Yaaaah to you!" said the Angel behind me.

I crossed the meadow and went along the little stream to the garden on the side opposite to Angel's house. There was a big hole in the wire of the fence here, and you could climb through as I did now. The man who worked in the next-door garden every morning had said it was all right. His name was Herr Wawra, and he was caretaker of the villa next door. He lived there by himself because the owners of the house had gone away. "Off to the West, that's where they went," said Herr Wawra.

"Were they scared of the Russians?" I asked.

Herr Wawra nodded. "Huh! Them! Scared of the Russians and the Yanks and the French—scared stiff of everyone!" He looked thoughtfully up at the blue sky. "And right they were to be scared too!" he told me, pointing to the house. "See that house? They took it off old Herr Goldmann. Jakob Goldmann, Senior. Stole his sugar refinery too! They took everything the Jews had away from them!" Herr Wawra laughed. "So now they see their fine friend Hitler is losing the war, and they're scared stiff of the Jews coming back to knock their Nazi heads together!"

My mother had strictly forbidden me to discuss such matters with anyone, so my voice trembled slightly as I said, "Herr Wawra, the Jews won't be coming back. Hitler shut them up in concentration camps and they're being killed, every single one!"

"Hush, child, hush! Hold your tongue!" whispered Herr Wawra. "Don't talk like that! Children shouldn't know about such things."

"But I do know," I said. "I've got an uncle in the SS, a real big shot. He's at the Führer's headquarters. He had a quarrel with my mother once about the Jews, and he said the Jews were all going up through the concentration camp chimneys. And when he said that he went 'Ffft!' "

"Nice sort of uncle you have, I must say!" muttered Herr Wawra. He took an apple out of his trouser pocket and gave it to me. I said thank you and went back to the hole in the fence.

Herr Wawra followed me. "Herr Goldmann will be coming back, all the same," he said. "You wait and see, child, you wait and see!"

After my visit to Herr Wawra I went back to the garden gate again, to see if the Commissioner had gone for his walk yet. But he did not seem to be planning a walk today; he was throwing sticks for his dogs to fetch.

The rightful owners—My revenge

One day I was swinging on the big garden gate, holding on to its iron railings and pushing off with both feet. The gate swung open, shot across to the fence carrying me with it, banged into the iron spears, swung back and clicked shut. I pushed off again. The gate swung open and shot across to the fence with me again. At that moment a car drove up and stopped outside our garden. Cars were not a very common sight these days, least of all private cars, but this one was a private car, a black Mercedes. A boy and a girl got out of it. The girl was a little older than me, and the boy was quite small, about six or seven years old. They both stared at me. I kept swinging vigorously on the gate, making the fence of spears rock. The gravel crunched as the gate swung back and forth.

"Hey, you, stop it!" said the boy. "You'll break our gate!"

I let go of the garden gate so suddenly that I fell over, and the gate hit me on the head.

The boy looked at me with interest. "Did you hurt yourself?" he asked.

I did not answer him. I stood up and brushed the dirt off my knees.

A woman got out of the car, a pretty woman wearing lovely clothes. Then a man got out, went to the back and took out two suitcases and some boxes. He put them down on the pavement, said "Heil Hitler!," got into the car and drove off.

The woman picked up the suitcases, one in each hand, and walked into the garden. The girl was carrying two of the boxes, and the boy picked up another one. They went after the woman. There was still one cardboard carton left standing on the pavement, so I picked it up and followed the three of them.

The boy turned around. "Hey, you!" he said to me. "Where are our garden gnomes?"

I did not reply.

"Mama, the garden gnomes have gone," cried the boy. "They're all gone!"

"Don't get so worked up, Gerald," said the woman. "More things have gone than a few garden gnomes!" And she smiled at me. She had a merry face.

"The gnomes are all right," I said. "They're over in the meadow behind the house."

It turned out that the woman was old Frau von Braun's daughter-in-law and the children were old Frau von Braun's grandchildren. Their names were Hildegard and Gerald. They were really all three of them supposed to be going to old Frau von Braun's place in the Tyrol, but there were no trains running, and the car that was supposed to take them there was not available either. Moreover, young Frau von Braun did not want to go and stay with her mother-in-law at all. Her husband, old Frau von Braun's son, was dead, and young Frau von Braun had been living in an apartment in the city, but the building next door was bombed, and now her apartment had no window panes or electric light and there were bomb splinters in all the furniture. So she had decided to move into her mother-in-law's villa.

Young Frau von Braun was all right. She understood about my father, too, and said she would have liked to hide her own husband, only he would not hear of it. He thought it was a very fine, grand thing to wear Hitler's uniform and get into a German plane and shoot down English planes. And now he was dead, which, said Frau von Braun, was all that old dragon's fault. She meant old Frau von Braun, who had never taught her son to have more sense.

So young Frau von Braun was all right. But I was not so keen on the children. They kept saying "our garden" and "our house" and "our trees." And when they talked about the uncles in the Uncles' Room they called them "our grandfather" and "our Uncle Friedrich." They were allowed to take the linen dust covers off the armchairs and unroll the carpets, too, and they had the keys to the two summerhouses in the garden.

Next morning I was making my round of the garden fences, and there was the Angel waiting for me by the wire fence again, doll's pram and all. Today she was wearing a particularly grand dress, a velvet one, with a lilac ribbon in her hair, and her curls were newly washed and shining. It was a long time since my hair had been washed; we had no soap. I said "Yaaaah!"

Suddenly I found Gerald beside me, going "Yaaaah!" at the Angel too.

The Angel patted her curls, smiled and lisped, "Hullo, Gerald! Where've you been all this time? Have you come to stay? Are you going to have to live with *her* now?" And the Angel pointed at me.

Gerald went "Yaaaah!" again.

The Angel, still pointing at me, said, "She keeps saying she has a doll's pram, but she hasn't really!"

"Of course she has!" shouted Gerald. "I've seen it! It's in the salon, but it's so valuable we're not allowed to take it out in the garden. It's got diamonds and pearls all over it!"

The Angel stared at us, pushing her black cat back into the pram as usual.

"Let that cat out!" said Gerald.

"Let that cat out!" I shouted.

"It's my cat!" said the Angel.

Then Hildegard came and joined us, and so did my sister, and suddenly we were all climbing over the wire fence. We knocked over the doll's pram, and took the doll's dress off the cat. The cat scratched us; I expect we were hurting it, but the doll's dress was a tight fit, and it was difficult to get it off. Finally the cat was free, and it ran away. It had a lame leg.

The Angel stood and watched us, howling. "That's my cat!" she sobbed. "You're mean and horrible! It's my cat; it's my pram! Mine, mine!"

The Angel ran off towards her house. We threw fir cones after her, shouting, "Silly old Angel! Feeble old Angel! Mummy's little darling! Go on, then! Go and tell Mummy!"

Then we got back over the fence and ran for the house, because we were frightened of the Angel's mother—the Archangel we called her. We took refuge in the Uncles' Room, and my sister told the von Braun children how to play Guess the Uncle.

Frau von Braun's grandchildren were all right too.

The Commissioner—Broken glass— Venison and goulash

That afternoon the Forestry Commissioner from over the road and his wife did leave their villa, but not just to take a walk. A car came, and they loaded suitcases and boxes into it. They put more suitcases on the roof of the car, tying them in place with cords. The Commissioner's wife was sniffing into a handkerchief. We stood at the garden gate, watching curiously. When the Commissioner had packed all the cases and boxes and cartons into the car, he came over to us. "Will you fetch your mama, please?" he asked Gerald.

Gerald called to young Frau von Braun, who was in the

garden. "Mama, Mama! It's the Commissioner. He wants something."

Frau von Braun came to the gate, and the Commissioner bowed to her. "I have come to say goodbye, Frau von Braun," he said. He swallowed. "I've shot my two dogs, my faithful friends—given them the *coup de grâce!*" He pointed to the car. "We're taking our things—the things we shan't be able to do without." His voice dropped to a whisper. "It's all over now, you see. Absolutely over! They'll never be able to hold out now." And he whispered, even more softly, "I have reliable information that the Russians are in Purkersdorf already!" He shook Frau von Braun's hand. "Take your children and escape while you can, dear lady! The Russians are terrible!"

"My dear sir, everything is terrible," said Frau von Braun.

The Commissioner shook his head, and went back to the car. It drove off. The Commissioner's wife waved to us, sobbing.

At last we could get into the house over the road!

Gerald and Hildegard were the first to cross the road and climb the fence. There was no one anywhere in sight. I ran over the road after them. I got stuck as I climbed the fence, and tore my dress on it—the dress that made me look like a flowered quilt. I tumbled into the currant bushes behind the fence, and crawled over to Hildegard and Gerald on all fours.

We were still waiting for my sister, who was standing at our garden gate, talking to old Herr Wawra. Finally, he went back into his own garden, and my sister ran across the road, jumped over the fence, and landed on the other side with us.

"Old Wawra gave me an apple," she said, taking it out of her skirt pocket. She had a bite and passed it on to me. I took a bite too, and passed it on to Gerald, and we all four shared the apple, making sure that no one took too large a bite out of it. Then we crept over to the cellar window.

The cellar window was open, but it turned out to be too small for us to get through. Besides, there was a drop of at least three metres from the window down into the cellar.

We crept round to the back of the house, where there was a glassed-in veranda with a pear tree growing close to it. We climbed the tree and jumped onto the veranda roof. From the roof, you could scramble onto a balcony if you were nimble enough. Gerald made it to the balcony, and then found that the door there was locked. He looked through its glass panes. "The key's there, on the inside," he said.

There was a flowerpot with a dead plant in it on the balcony. Gerald picked it up.

"He's going to break the glass," said my sister.

"Oh, Gerald, no! You mustn't!" cried Hildegard.

"All the window panes are broken back in the city," said my sister.

I nodded. Gerald picked up the flowerpot and threw it at the glass. The glass shattered, and the flowerpot fell inside the room. Gerald put his hand carefully through the hole in the glass, unlocked the door, and disappeared into the house.

We waited, while the veranda roof creaked and groaned under our weight. Gerald appeared at the window just above the veranda, grinning, waved to us, and opened the window. We all climbed into the house.

The place was cold inside, and smelled of rotten potatoes. We explored the rooms, feeling rather disappointed. Another Uncles' Room with a piano—there were a few aunts scattered among the uncles here. Another room full of books. No linen covers on the chairs in the salon here, though. We went downstairs to the ground floor, and found the kitchen. There was a mouldy loaf of bread left on the kitchen table.

"Oh, let's go home. There isn't anything interesting here," said my sister.

There was a very tall, broad cupboard in the kitchen. Hildegard opened it—and then we stood there transfixed, rooted to the spot and staring. We had never seen anything like it in our lives! The cupboard was full of preserving jars. Jars of cherry preserve, and apricot preserve, and other jars that shone pale brown and dark brown. The jars had labels decorated with sprigs of flowers, saying things like *Venison à la jardinière, 1944* and *Ragout of Venison Esterhazy, 1943* and *Liver sausage with goose liver.* There were jars of green beans and jars of tomatoes too.

"Oh, my goodness!" whispered Hildegard. "Oh, my goodness me!"

"They did all right for themselves, didn't they?" I breathed.

There was a big check tablecloth on the kitchen table. Hildegard swept the mouldy loaf of bread off the table, and I removed the cloth. We spread it out on the floor, put as many of the preserving jars on it as it could hold, and then knotted its corners together. It was heavy, but my sister and Hildegard could just about manage to carry it between them. Gerald found an old shopping bag and filled it with jars of liver sausage. "I say, I *say!*" he almost groaned. "Liver sausage! Liver sausage . . . let's hope they didn't put any marjoram in it, I like it better plain!"

I fetched a cloth with a tasselled fringe from the dining room, loaded it up with jars labelled venison (cooked in various ways), and knotted the corners of this cloth together too. We climbed out of the kitchen window, easing our loot through the window very, very carefully, and closed it behind us.

It proved impossible to get our bundles over the garden fence.

"We'll just have to leave the stuff here," said Hildegard, discouraged. "I suppose it doesn't really belong to us, anyway. . . ."

"What? Leave all this liver sausage here? Are you nuts?" Gerald tapped his forehead.

I went over to the garden gate, which had a round brass knob on the outside, and an iron latch on the inside. Just on the off chance, I pressed down the latch, and the gate opened.

"That's what's known as more luck than brains," whispered my sister.

I looked cautiously up and down the road. There was no one about. "Come on!" I cried.

We ran across the road, dragging our huge bundles behind us, hearing the jars clink as they knocked together.

We reached our own garden, slammed the gate behind us, lugged our burdens up the gravel path, and climbed the four steps to the front door, panting for breath. We had never carried anything so heavy before.

My mother and Frau von Braun were standing at the doorway.

"Where have you been all this time?" asked my mother.

"What on earth have you got there?" asked Frau von Braun.

We took our loot into the hall and untied the corners of the tablecloths. Gerald turned the shopping bag upside down, and jars of liver sausage went rolling across the floor.

Obviously there was nothing to do but to tell the truth, so I simply said, "We stole them."

My mother and Frau von Braun stared at me. I felt uncomfortable. I began to worry: surely they wouldn't say we had to put all those jars back again?

"There's liver sausage in the little ones," said Gerald. "Real liver sausage—with bits of goose liver in it!"

My mother and Frau von Braun stopped staring at me and started staring at the jars instead. They knelt down on the floor and picked them up, one by one.

"Venison à la jardinière, 1944," my mother read.

"Liver sausage with tongue . . . liver sausage with bacon," whispered Frau von Braun.

"We found them in the Leinfellners' house," said Hildegard, pointing to the street. "In the kitchen cupboard. Well, the Leinfellners have gone anyway, haven't they?"

Then Frau von Braun began to laugh, and so did my mother, and they laughed till the tears were streaming down their cheeks.

"Liver sausage with tongue, Herr Leinfellner! Heil Hitler, Herr Leinfellner!" cried Frau von Braun, picking up a jar of venison. "We must hold out till the day of victory dawns, that's what Herr Leinfellner always used to say! Not too difficult holding out when you have plenty of venison in the larder, eh, Herr Leinfellner?"

My mother was kneeling on the tasselled cloth; she had stopped laughing now. She was looking at a two-litre preserving jar full of veal. *"Schnitzel in Madeira sauce, 1944,"* she said. She shook her head. "And we've been living on potatoes, potatoes, and more potatoes!"

The uniform—The SS men—Stolen cigarettes

About midday some German soldiers came marching along the road past our garden, coming from the Wienerwald, northwest of Vienna. They were going towards the city, and they were followed by some Wehrmacht vehicles.

I was standing by the fence of iron spears with Hildegard. We waited to see if there were any more cars or trucks or soldiers coming, but that was the lot.

Herr Wawra was leaning on his garden gate, further down the road. "That's the last of them, children," he told us. "They're all gone now. Thank God, the war's over."

"Someone was saying on the radio that we must defend Vienna to our last breath," Hildegard said. "To our last breath, Herr Wawra!" But old Herr Wawra stuck to his guns. He shook his head. "They're all gone now, all gone," he kept repeating.

"It's high time we burnt your uniform and paybook," my mother told my father. "We don't want the Russians finding them!"

My father limped up and down the salon, up and down. He kept trying to get the news on the radio, but the radio would only crackle and whistle. It was a very old set. Was it broken, or wasn't there any broadcasting station now? We did not know.

My father did not want to burn his uniform. "If the Germans come back and find me, and I don't have my paybook or my uniform, they'll hang me from the nearest tree!" he said.

"If the Germans come back and find you they'll hang you anyway, paybook or no paybook," said my mother. "That won't make any difference!"

However, she did not burn the uniform.

I looked out of the window. There was a car outside our garden gate, and four men in SS uniforms were coming up the gravel path towards the house.

My father went into the library, walking slowly as if he was not afraid. Frau von Braun closed the door behind him, leaned against it and whispered to my mother, "Do you think someone's informed against him . . . the Archangel or Herr Wawra, maybe?" I was going to say that Herr Wawra would never inform against my father when there was a knock at the front door. My mother took the library key out of the keyhole and put it in her apron pocket. Then she went to open the door.

"Keep your mouths shut!" Frau von Braun hissed at us. "Whatever they say, whatever they ask you, keep your mouths shut—understand?" We nodded.

But the SS men had not come for my father. They had a tin of clarified butter and a bag of potatoes, and they wanted my mother to cook fried potatoes for them. They even fetched some wood from the shed so that she could light the stove. Frau von Braun whispered to us again, "Remember—keep your mouths shut!"

The four SS men sat at the kitchen table and my mother fried a great mound of potatoes. The clarified butter foamed up in the pan and over the sides, sizzling on the hotplate of the stove. It made a horrible smell. The SS men ate and talked. They said Vienna was altogether undefended now.

"The city's as good as fallen already," said one of them.

Another man told us he came from Schleswig, which the Russians had occupied some time ago. And before the Russians came, his wife took both children and got out of the place. He said we'd better not stay here, and even offered to take us into the city so that we could take refuge in one of the big bunkers. My mother refused.

In between giving advice the SS men tried to talk to us children. They asked our names, and how old we were, and a lot of other questions. They must have thought us remarkably stupid children; we just sat huddled close together at the table, eating the leftover potatoes and not answering. We did not say a word, merely goggled. We goggled at the oilcloth on the table, we goggled at the SS men.

"Frightened out of their wits!" said one of them.

"Scared silly!" said another.

"My kids aren't like that," said the man whose wife had taken the children and got out of Schleswig. "Real little toughs, they are, game for anything! Nothing gets *them* down!" He sounded very proud.

"Come on, little girl, speak up!" said one of them coaxingly, stroking my hair.

But for one thing I had been forbidden to talk, and for another, I was beginning to enjoy this! I went on staring doggedly at the SS men.

Frau von Braun tried to lift her prohibition on talking. "Go on, then, dear, tell the gentleman your name. It's quite all right. . . ."

I told myself she could go on like that till the cows came home, but I did not say so, I just sat there goggling. My sister goggled too. Hildegard goggled. Gerald goggled.

The sight of us bothered the SS men. We made them feel

uncomfortable. They decided to set off; they had to get to Salzburg today, and they did not know which roads were still open, which bridges not yet blown up. They put their coats on, did up their leather belts, and said goodbye to Frau von Braun and my mother.

"Say goodbye nicely, children," my mother told us.

We stayed put, stuffing potatoes into our mouths, and I did my best to squint. The man with the wife who had got out of Schleswig looked pityingly at us. Then they left. We ran to the window and pressed our noses against the panes.

The SS men were getting into their car.

I took the library key out of my mother's apron pocket and ran off to see my father. I put my hand into the pocket of my flowered-quilt dress and down my neck, and produced two packets of cigarettes, one full and one half-full.

It is quite possible to goggle mindlessly at people while stealing cigarettes off the table at the same time. I was proud of myself. Hildegard and Gerald admired my prowess too, but my sister said, "That wasn't very nice of you. People shouldn't steal!"

"Why not?" I asked. "*You* helped steal the jars of venison and things!"

"That wasn't really stealing, because the Leinfellners aren't here any more, they've run away," said my sister. "But those soldiers gave you fried potatoes and were kind to us, so it was mean to steal from them." She appealed to my father. "It *is* mean to steal, Daddy, isn't it?"

My father was lying on the carpet, cigarette smoke curling out of his nostrils and hovering in the air. My father grinned. "Yes, of course, dear!" he said.

"There! See?" My sister dug her forefinger into my stomach. "Daddy says it's very mean too!"

My father smoked his cigarette, inhaling deeply. It was a long time since he had had a real cigarette. He had been rolling his own for days. My mother got the tobacco from a neighbour, Herr Zimmer, in return for one of the pairs of trousers she had been given, but Herr Zimmer's tobacco was damp and did not draw very well.

My father murmured, "It's mean to steal cigarettes. It's very mean to smoke stolen cigarettes. But it's even meaner to *have* cigarettes when other people have none left!"

"There! See?" I told my sister in turn, digging my forefinger into her stomach.

My father asked me to fetch him the hairpin which was on the desk. He did not have a proper cigarette holder. I gave him the hairpin, he stuck the lighted cigarette end into it, and like that he could smoke the cigarette down to a tiny stub without burning his fingers.

My mother came to call us to supper. "The last SS men are leaving Vienna!" she said. "This calls for a celebration!"

We had fried potatoes, venison *à la jardinière*, and apricot preserve.

The Stalin Organ—The Volkischer Beobachter— The mice—The headless doll

After our celebration supper my mother and Frau von Braun took mattresses and blankets and pillows down to the cellar. My father followed them, carrying the jars of venison and apricots and so on, and stacked them behind the cellar steps. They took our few shabby clothes down to the cellar too. They had decided that we children were all to sleep in the cellar tonight.

I didn't want to. I did not in the least want to go down to that cellar. It was not a safe cellar, it was a ridiculous cellar for a bomb shelter. It lay below the two terraces, the round one and the square one, and it was meant for storing potatoes and carrots, not for wartime. Why, just a quarter of a bomb would knock a cellar like that into the middle of next week. Besides, I'd had quite enough of cellars, even good safe ones. I had spent far too much time, far too often, in cellars. Cellars stink. Cellars are cold. Cellars are nasty.

"No!" I screamed. "You go! You go down to your silly old cellar! I'm staying up here!"

However, it was no use; I was forced to go down. My mother

tried to soothe me. "Come now, don't get upset!" she said. "It isn't bombs we're afraid of. I don't suppose there'll be any bombs dropped now, but there may be firing from the Russians tonight."

"What will they be firing?" asked my sister.

"Cannons, machine guns . . . oh, how should I know?" My mother shrugged her shoulders.

"I wonder if they've brought a Stalin Organ with them?" said Gerald.

"Heaven forbid! I hope not! Don't say such things!" said my mother.

The "Stalin Organ" was supposed to be the most terrible of all the Russian guns. It was impossible to picture it; no one knew exactly what the thing looked like, but it was rumoured to be a gigantic cannon with over a hundred mouths to fire deadly cannonballs full of nails and pieces of iron and rusty wire. Cannonballs that smashed and shot and burnt everything in sight.

So we were sent down to the cellar. Our mattresses were hard, and the cold and damp seeped up from the floor through them. Our blankets were thin and scratchy, and soon they too felt damp and cold.

The cellar walls were papered with newspaper just like our cellar in Hernals; old copies of the *Völkischer Beobachter*, or *People's Observer*, a very biased Nazi paper. It smelled the same too.

They had left the cellar door open, and put a lighted candle on the cellar steps. The candle flickered, throwing jerky shadows on the cellar roof and walls. The light trembled on the *Völkischer Beobachter* and I tried to read the newsprint above my head. But the letters were too small. Besides, the sheets of newspaper were upside down.

My sister lay beside me, asleep and snoring. She had adenoids. I had hated her adenoidal snoring ever since I could remember; it sometimes kept me awake at night.

I sat up and looked at Gerald. He was asleep, his thumb in his mouth, his blanket on the floor beside him. I looked at Hildegard. Hildegard was in the corner of the cellar beside me. I could not see her face, because the light did not reach that far.

"Are you asleep, Hildegard?" I called.

"I'm frightened!" whispered Hildegard.

"Of the Russians?"

"Of the mice."

"Are there mice here?"

"Don't know," whispered Hildegard. "There were lots of mice when we came to stay here in the summer a few years ago. We set traps, but we never caught a mouse. Not one."

I got up, took the candle from the cellar steps and put it down between our mattresses. Now I could see Hildegard's face and one of her hands, in which she was holding a funny pink thing.

"What's that?" I asked.

"I hold it when I'm going to sleep," said Hildegard. She passed me the pink thing. It was the body of a small doll, made of pink flannel, with a red dot of a navel embroidered on it.

"It's lost its head," I said.

"Not lost. Never had one," whispered Hildegard.

I looked at the pink doll's body. One leg was longer and fatter than the other, and its arms stood out from the square body like a signpost.

"Homemade?" I asked.

Hildegard nodded. "My mummy made it. She was going to leave the doll's head till last, because that's the most difficult part. But then the telegram came to say my daddy's plane had been shot down and he was dead, so she stopped making the doll."

I gave Hildegard the pink object back.

"There's an old rag in the gas meter cupboard," I said. "It used to be a pair of pink knickers. We could make a head out of that tomorrow. With button eyes, and there's still the fringe of that shawl my mama unravelled. We can use that for hair. It'll look good and real!"

Hildegard shook her head. "No," she said. "I want to leave it as it is."

I took my blanket and pillow and lay down on Hildegard's mattress beside her. We could keep warmer that way.

"I'm so scared of the mice," said Hildegard.

"I was once scared stiff of a crack in the ceiling," I told her.

"But there isn't any crack in the ceiling here," murmured Hildegard.

"I bet all the mice starved to death ages ago," I said, blowing out the candle.

My mother came to the cellar door, and climbed down a few steps, trying to be quiet, but the cellar steps creaked. "Everyone asleep? Good!" she said under her breath. Then she went up the steps again and closed the cellar door behind her.

"I like that!" I said indignantly to Hildegard. "They make us go down to this cold, dark hole and *they* stay up in their nice warm beds. Mean, I call it!"

"No, they only want to be sure we're safe," whispered Hildegard.

I sat up again, wrapped the blanket round me, straightened Hildegard's blanket, and said, "Well, suppose they get shot by the Russians upstairs, and we're left down here?"

"Be quiet! Oh, do be quiet!" said Hildegard. "I'm asleep!"

Cake—The gnomes' school— The man with the brown leather cap

When I woke up, daylight was coming in through the cellar window, casting a pattern of black bars on my blanket. I was alone in the cellar. I jumped up, climbed the cellar steps and ran to the kitchen, keeping my ears pricked for unusual sounds as I went. Could I hear footsteps? Someone talking a foreign language? Firing a gun? Were the Russians here?

But there were no Russians. My grandfather was there instead, sitting in the kitchen with the others. He had brought a cake, a real cake. A sponge cake with currants in it, and chocolate icing. Grandfather had given Herr Huber, the confectioner, his gold watch, and in return Herr Huber had given Grandfather the cake. There were only three pieces left, and they were mine; the others had already finished theirs. I ate my cake fast, cramming it into my mouth, gobbling. I wanted to get it finished before my sister could ask me to give her a little bit.

Grandfather did not believe us when we told him the Russians might arrive any minute. "That's as may be," he said, chuckling. "Every day people say the Russians are coming, but they're not here yet!"

The cake was not all that Grandfather had brought. He had some other things salvaged from the rubble. He spent all day digging in the rubble now; he had nothing better to do.

"Grandfather, you really must stop it, you know," my mother told him. "It's dangerous digging in those rubble heaps. The whole lot could easily fall in."

Grandfather nodded. "You're right, it could easily fall in." But he didn't sound as if he would mind one way or the other.

I went out to the meadow behind the house, with Hildegard and Gerald, and we began playing a game with the garden gnomes. We stood them up in two rows and played school with them. The one with the whetstone was always at the bottom of the class. Hildegard was the teacher, and I put on different voices for the various gnome pupils. My favourite part was the stupid one with the whetstone. Hildegard scolded him. "You naughty boy, give me that knife this minute! What are you doing with a knife in class?"

I replied in the gnome's voice, "I think you're crazy, miss!"

Hildegard wanted to be a kind teacher, and tried to talk nicely to the naughty gnome with the whetstone. I disagreed; I thought she ought to be a nasty, cross teacher, to make the game more fun. As for Gerald, he refused to play, because we had said he was to be school caretaker, and he didn't think that was a good part. He walked up and down the rows of garden gnomes, kicking them over. One of them broke its nose. "Who cares about you and your silly games?" said Gerald crossly. "I'm always supposed to be the caretaker, or the housekeeper, or the baby. I'm not playing with you any more!" He went over to the garden fence in search of the Angel.

I stood the garden gnomes up again, Hildegard collected the broken bits of nose, and we tried to put it together. But it was no good; there were too many little bits of plaster broken off. Suddenly we heard a humming sound in the air, a loud and dangerous sound, a sound we had never heard before. A plane appeared above the fir trees near Herr Wawra's fence. All of a sudden it was huge, and very low. It was above us, it was everywhere, it cast a huge terrifying shadow over the meadow. We stood perfectly still.

Now the plane was above the roof of the Archangel's house. It made a loop and came back, flying very low, at an odd angle in the sky. It was not really a large plane.

I could see inside the plane. There was a man sitting there, just one man, wearing a brown leather cap. The plane flew over Herr Wawra's garden and came back again, even lower, even louder.

I thought: There's a man with a brown leather cap sitting in that plane. There's a man with a brown leather cap sitting in that plane. Over and over again: There's a man with a brown leather cap sitting in that plane.

I kept thinking this to stop myself from being frightened. It was a good thought to cling to. I was frightened of planes, but not of men with brown leather caps, since men with brown leather caps had never done anything to hurt me.

I saw Gerald running back to the house from the Archangel's fence, keeping low. I saw Hildegard run for the house too. She stumbled over a garden gnome and almost fell.

I did not run. I stayed put.

The plane came back. Its shadow reached out for me, and the air hissed as the plane swooped past. It had wheels underneath.

Apparently all the others were standing at the kitchen window, shouting to me to run back to the house at once, but I did not hear them, probably because of the noise of the plane. Then my father came out of the house, limping as he ran towards me, seized my arm and dragged me back to the door with him. I stumbled into the hall.

My father slammed the door. "Are you crazy?" he cried. "What on earth did you think you were doing, standing there like a moonstruck idiot? Do you want to get yourself killed?"

I said, "There was a man with a brown leather cap in that plane."

They did not understand. They were all shouting at once, telling me there were men in all the planes, men who shot guns, men who dropped bombs, and there was a man behind every cannon that fired a cannonball, and it made no difference whatever if their caps were brown or green!

I kept my mouth shut, because they were so cross and angry, even Grandfather. But I knew quite well that they were wrong.

A hero—A hoard of beans and noodles—
The handcart

I sat down by the kitchen window and pretended to be looking at the garden. I listened to the things my grandfather and my
father and Frau von Braun were saying. My mother did not join
in; she was sitting beside the big stove, crying a little, and she
kept on blowing her nose.

Grandfather was bewildered now, and did not know what to
do. The man in the brown leather cap had finally convinced even
him that the Russians really might arrive any minute.

"You can't leave now!" said my father. "You'll have to stay
here. They'll shoot you on sight in the streets."

Grandfather was frightened of the journey home, and he
would have liked to stay, but he was even more frightened of
Grandmother. "I can't leave Juli on her own," he said.

My father lost his temper. "Oh, for God's sake!" he shouted.
"What good will you be to your Juli if you're dead within the
hour?"

"Herr Göth, it's madness to think of walking for two hours
through the streets just now!" cried Frau von Braun. She tried
again. "Herr Göth, you don't have to be a hero."

Grandfather buttoned up his coat and put his hat on. "Well,
I don't suppose this would be the first time a man's become a
hero out of fright! Anyway, I must get back to Juli."

And Grandfather left. I watched him through the kitchen
window as he closed the garden gate and disappeared on the
other side of the iron spears.

Grandfather will be passing the Archangel's gate now, I
thought. Now he'll have reached Atariastrasse. Now he'll be passing the Party Centre. Now he's at the Number 43 tram terminus.
Now he'll be going past the bomb craters in the Alszeile.

But I realised that Grandfather could not be walking as fast as I was thinking, so I began again: He'll be going past the Archangel's house now. Five more paces to reach the yellow house.

Thirty paces along the fence. One—two—three . . .

Faster, Grandfather! Oh, do go faster!

Now he'll be passing the old inn with the glass veranda.

Run, Grandfather! Please run!

I heard the hum of a plane, not very close, quite a long way off. Grandfather would be quite a long way off by now too. I hoped it was my man with the brown leather cap sitting in that plane.

The Angel's mother came over and said we must shut the children indoors, because of planes flying low over the gardens. One had been over their garden, she said. It was dreadful, terrible, we had no idea how terrible.

Oh, thanks for nothing, Archangel, I thought. Stop it, do! That was *my* airman in that plane. I know him better than you do. Shut up, Archangel.

The Archangel did not shut up. My mother stopped sniffling and told her about me and the plane.

Oh, Mama, why don't *you* shut up too? Grandfather's on his way home, and it's a long way to go, Mama. Is he still in the Alszeile, or has he got to the Hauptstrasse in Hernals now? I've lost track, and it's important. There are big, tall buildings in the Hernalser Hauptstrasse. Once he gets there he can keep in the shelter of their walls. Perhaps there *are* some planes with people in them who like shooting, after all.

My mother stopped talking, not because I wanted her to, but because the Archangel was fluttering excitedly round the kitchen, telling her a fascinating item of news. ". . . And there's something else I was going to tell you! People have broken into the stores at the NSV Home!" NSV stood for *Nationalsozialistische Volkswohlfahrt,* the National Socialist People's Welfare organisation. "They've smashed down the gate and got in. They're acting like savages. Stealing things! Looting! Dreadful, isn't it? Disgusting! I never heard of such a thing! I call it . . . I call it . . ." But the Archangel ran out of words to express her indignation.

"Where is the NSV Home?" asked my mother.

"Down in Atariastrasse, second on the left," said Frau von Braun, putting on her coat.

"We'll take the children," my mother decided.

"Put your coat on!" said my father.

The Archangel's eyes widened and her jaw dropped. "Where are you going? What are you going to do?" The Archangel stared at us. "You're not going to join in too!"

"Indeed we are!" said my mother.

"Do you mean . . . really?" The Archangel was incredulous.

"Yes, that's right, we're going on a looting expedition!" said my father. "Looting, my dear Frau Engel!"

The Archangel stopped staring, fluttered about some more, and cried, "Wait for me, wait for me! I'm coming too!"

We hurried down Neuwaldegger Strasse to the NSV Home, with the Archangel behind us. As we passed the Archangel's garden we heard the Angel screeching that she didn't want to be left alone. She made as much noise as if she were being roasted alive. The Archangel took no notice at all.

The big, dark brown gate of the NSV Home was open; its lock had been broken. A man came along the long, dark alley leading from the NSV Home to the gate. He was carrying two big blue paper bags and a brown linen one.

"The stores are round the back, in the yard," he told us.

The storeroom was a big place which had probably once been the main public room of an inn, where people going for Sunday outings would drop in. It was full of tall wooden shelves. There were stacks of big blue and brown bags and white cartons on the shelves, and people were scurrying about among them. I was surprised to see how many people were still left around here. I had thought we and the two Angels and Herr Wawra and Herr Zimmer were about the last, but there were at least fifty people here, acting very strangely. They were running up and down the aisles between the shelves, tearing holes in the blue paper bags, knocking piles of white cartons to the floor. They cut open the brown linen bags with knives, looked inside, and then moved on. Some might be carrying a couple of blue bags, only to throw them down again, snatch up a brown bag, run to the door, fling the brown bag away in a corner, and go back for three white boxes instead. Noodles and beans and peas were trickling out onto the floor through the holes that had been made in the bags. There were other things which I couldn't identify; for instance, there were piles of small, grey objects, which tasted very salty, but nice. And there were little, dark brown threadlike things, mixed up with the split noodles and peas. I tasted them as well, and discovered that they were dehydrated onion.

The floor was soon ankle-deep in beans and peas and noodles, and they kept on trickling out of the bags. They crunched whenever you moved, but it was impossible to avoid treading on them; the whole floor was covered. I enjoyed walking over the beans and peas and pasta. They made a lovely scrunching noise.

My father was wheeling a handcart into the store. A thin old lady followed him in, shouting and screeching, "You scoundrel, you! What do you think you're doing? That's my handcart! Give me back my handcart this minute! You can't go off with my handcart like that. . . ."

The handcart scrunched through the noodles. "You'll be getting your blasted handcart back!" shouted my father. My mother and Frau von Braun loaded up the handcart with blue bags and brown bags and white cartons, and two big cans of cooking oil, until it was carrying all it could hold.

My father pulled the handcart from in front, my mother and Frau von Braun pushed from behind, Hildegard and I held the mountain of blue and brown bags steady on one side, and my sister and Gerald supported it on the other.

Like this, we made our slow and laborious way over the carpet of noodles. A young woman tried to dispute possession of the handcart with us, saying that she lived next door to the old lady who owned the cart, so she had more right to it than we did. The old lady herself was still standing at the door of the storeroom shouting, "No! No! No one else is having my cart! Nobody! Give it back! It's mine, mine!"

My father was trying to get the handcart through the door of the storeroom. The old lady stood in the doorway, her arms braced against the frame. My father let go of the cart, took the old lady under the armpits and dragged her out of the doorway. The old lady kicked out, her legs dangling in the air. She shouted, "Brutes! Riffraff! Put me down! This isn't your property. It belongs to the NSV! No one's allowed to take it! Nor my handcart either, nor my handcart either!"

My father carried the struggling old lady across the yard and put her down in a flower bed, among some yellow and purple crocuses. He came back and took hold of the handcart again.

I giggled, because the old lady looked so funny in the crocuses.

"There's nothing to laugh about!" my mother said, reproving me.

"Serves her right, greedy old thing," said my sister.

"It's not her fault," said my mother.

We made slow progress. The mountain of bags wobbled, and some of them fell off. We had to reload the bags and cans. At last we got in through our garden gate. Once on the gravel path, the cart decided it had had enough, and lost a wheel. We carried the cart bodily into the house, and threw the wheel into the ivy.

The salty things—The Archangel's loot— Old Herr Wawra's loot—The strange noise

My parents and Frau von Braun went down to the cellar with their blue, brown, and white treasures, to add them to our secret hoard of preserving jars from the Leinfellners' villa. They were very excited, and their cheeks were flushed. They had peas and noodles! They had sugar and dehydrated onions! They had beans and oil!

"We'll put the bags of beans over there!" they said. And: "The sugar can go under the cellar steps!" And: "Let's stack the bags of peas in the corner!"

It sounded as if they were really saying, "We'll make it yet! We'll survive!"

I took some of the grey, salty little objects out of one of the white cartons, and let them drop into my pocket.

"Goodness, no!" cried my mother. "You can't eat those raw. That's dried beef broth!"

"I like them raw," I said. I left the house and went across the meadow to see old Herr Wawra.

Old Herr Wawra was tidying the garden paths with a metal rake, as he did every day, though there was no one to walk along the paths and mess them up.

"Was that you I saw coming along the road with a cart full of bags?" Herr Wawra asked me, leaning his rake against a tree trunk.

I nodded. I took some of the grey things from my pocket and offered them to old Herr Wawra. "Dried beef broth," I explained.

"Beef broth is wet!" he said.

"Not this. This is dried," I told him.

Old Herr Wawra took one of the grey objects, examined it, rubbed it between his horny thumb and forefinger. "More like a bit of snot, if you ask me!" old Herr Wawra muttered.

"Try it! It's nice," I said.

Herr Wawra was reluctant to try. "Beef broth would never dry up to look like snot!" he insisted.

"Yes, honestly, it does!" I said. Though I was not so sure myself by now; snot does taste rather nice and salty.

I told Herr Wawra about the NSV Home and the bags of food. The Archangel broke into the middle of our conversation, coming along the road wailing at the top of her voice, and followed by the Angel, wailing too. The Archangel had a brown bag in one hand and a blue one in the other, but they were both empty, fluttering at the Archangel's sides like wings.

Herr Wawra and I went out into the road to meet the Archangel.

"I was coming to tell you!" sobbed the Archangel. "The food's all gone! Already! All stolen! Nothing left!" She waved the empty bags at us, and a few noodles and peas fell out on the pavement.

"But the stores were still quite full!" I said.

"Oh, yes," said the Archangel, snuffling. "But then, well, I wanted thinner noodles, and I was looking for thinner noodles, and my bag of sugar got torn, and some great lout came along and just took my bag of beans away, and then . . . and then . . . people are so mean . . . then . . ."

The Archangel stopped. Her thin, straight yellow hair was hanging limp around her face, and her mouth was going all funny shapes. She looked at us with her mouth wide open and working, and tears running down her cheeks.

"Well, what did happen then?" asked old Herr Wawra.

The Archangel's mouth went back to normal. "Suddenly

everybody was gone," she said, "and so were all the bags and boxes and cans of things. Except the floor—the floor's all covered with the stuff, noodles and peas and sugar and so on. Ankle-deep, it is!"

"What do you mean, the floor?" Old Herr Wawra did not understand.

I told him how people had gone around making holes in the bags, so that the food had trickled out.

"Disgusting!" said old Herr Wawra.

"But I had to make holes in the bags too," said the Archangel. "Because there weren't any labels, nothing to show what was in them, and I wanted thinner noodles!"

"Well, you cow! You silly cow!" said Herr Wawra. He went back into his garden.

The Archangel, offended, went back to her own house too, still clutching the empty bags.

Old Herr Wawra came out of his garden gate again, with his wheelbarrow and a shovel. "Peas, beans, all that good food!" he was muttering. "Lying about the floor! What a wicked waste— can't have that! I'm off to get some."

I wanted to go back to the NSV Home with Herr Wawra, but my mother, who happened to be looking out of the kitchen window just then, would not let me. I climbed the fence of spears and watched Herr Wawra disappear in the direction of the NSV stores.

Some time later he came back, pushing his wheelbarrow very carefully up the street. It was full to the brim. There was sugar glistening among the noodles, and shreds of onion curled around the peas. Herr Wawra wheeled the barrow to the little summer-house in his garden and tipped its contents out there. Then he went back to the NSV Home for another load.

Old Herr Wawra made the journey at least nine times, until the summerhouse was quite full. Finally he stopped; he was tired. "The NSV Home is still full of the stuff!" he said.

I crawled through the fence and went over to his summer-house to see his mingled treasures. I let them run through my fingers. "You'll never be able to cook this," I said. "It'd taste of sugar, and that would be nasty. And noodles only take twenty minutes to cook, and beans take hours and hours!"

Old Herr Wawra sat down on the garden seat outside the summerhouse. He took several crumpled pieces of paper out of his coat pocket and smoothed them out flat. "Clever, aren't you?" he said. "You just keep your mouth shut and help me sort this lot out instead!"

He put the pieces of paper down on the seat beside him, and asked me to get a shovelful of the mixed beans and noodles and stuff from the summerhouse.

I brought him a shovelful of the mixture, and tipped it into his lap. Then we began sorting it out. We put the noodles on one piece of paper, the dehydrated onion on another, the peas on another and the beans on another.

I pointed to the summerhouse. "It'll take us a hundred years to finish this job!"

"I shan't live that long!" said Herr Wawra. "Nor will you!"

The biggest heap was noodles, and the smallest was peas.

"I could bring you a full bag of peas from our cellar," I offered, though I was not sure if my mother would let me give him one.

"I don't need a full bag," said Herr Wawra. "I'm an old man, and old people don't eat much."

A gentle spring breeze rose, blowing shreds of dehydrated onion off the garden seat. I retrieved them, scraping them up off the gravel path. I fetched another shovelful of the mixture. Old Herr Wawra's trousers were covered with white sugar.

Gerald came over to the fence.

"You've got to come in," he shouted.

"I'm sorting this stuff," I said.

"You go on home," said Herr Wawra. "I can manage on my own."

I shook my head, squatted down beside him again and went on sorting.

"One for each person and one for the pot!" Gerald teased me, going away.

I spent a long time helping to sort out the mixture. My feet went to sleep; there were pins and needles in my toes and heels. Soon it would be midday. Suddenly old Herr Wawra stopped sorting. He listened. "I can hear something," he said.

I could not hear anything.

"I can, though," said Herr Wawra. He shook the mixture in his lap onto a piece of paper, brushed the sugar dust off his trouser legs, and we went to the garden gate.

Now I could hear the sound too. It was a strange sound—

hollow, soft, indistinct—made up of many different noises put together.

"Horses," said old Herr Wawra. "And carts." And then: "The Russians are coming!"

I had been hoping the Russians would come for weeks—because of my father, and the Nazis, and a general feeling that it was time something different happened. And now here they were. I felt my heart beating in my throat, not in my chest, at the sound of the hollow, indistinct noise that was coming closer and closer. We could make out voices now. The noise grew much louder—an unusual noise, a strange noise. Then they turned out of the Hohenstrasse and began coming down our road. Horses and carts, with Russians riding in them. I still could not see any details; I could only make out a long column of horses and carts and Russians. I could tell from the noise that it must stretch a long, long way back beyond the corner of the road. The horses and carts and Russians were all a sort of yellowish grey.

I remembered the SS man's wife, the one who had taken her children and got out of Schleswig, and I remembered how the Russians were supposed to cut women's breasts off, and I could not help thinking of those women, all cut up into little bits and pickled. And I heard the Forestry Commissioner saying, "The Russians are terrible!"

Old Herr Wawra bent down and told me, "I need some soap powder!"

Why on earth did he want soap powder just now?

"Or anyway, a bit of household soap. Have you got any household soap?" asked old Herr Wawra.

I was still staring at the Russians. "Why do you want soap?"

"I'm going to turn out the bedroom—I must get it all bright and clean!" He pointed to the approaching column of Russians, and spoke right into my ear, making my head ring. "The Russians have arrived, so old Herr Goldmann will be coming back now! Fancy that—old Herr Goldmann! I must get his bed made, and scrub the floor. He'll be tired."

Well, I thought, the Russians are coming and old Herr Wawra has gone off his head!

"No, we haven't got any soap!" I shouted.

I ran back to our own garden gate.

My mother came out to meet me. "Wherever have you

been?" she shouted. She seized my hand and ran back to the house with me, crying, "The Russians are coming!"

"Yes, I know," I said. "With horses and carts. They've just turned into this road."

"If you ever run off again just when the Russians are coming, you'll be sorry!" yelled my mother.

White sheets—The uniform—
The uncles who changed size—
Knocking on the door—Fair hair and dark hair

My mother tried to get me inside the house, and I began to howl, clinging to the door handle. My mother tried to pry my fingers loose, gasping that I must be right out of my mind, and no wonder, but all the same I must go down to the cellar, or the Russians would get me! My father came and removed my fingers from the door handle, picked me up and carried me to the cellar door. I struggled frantically, howling the whole time. I was not quite sure just why I was howling; it was something to do with my fear of cellars, and something to do with old Herr Wawra, who was still standing at his garden gate expecting Herr Goldmann to turn up.

My father abruptly dropped me. I had kicked his poor, infected shins in my struggles. I landed on the floor and stopped howling.

"All right, don't go down to the cellar, then!" said my mother. "But you must stay in the house!" She pushed the big bolt across the inside of the front door.

I nodded.

Hildegard, Gerald, my sister, and Frau von Braun were down in the cellar. My sister called up, "Mummy, Daddy, come down!" Her voice was very frightened.

My father limped down to the cellar. I went into the salon

with my mother, and we looked out at the road. Out there the carts were going by, greyish-yellow wooden carts, drawn by small, grey horses. There were soldiers sitting in the carts, wearing uniforms of a dirty yellow colour. As far as I could see there were soldiers and horses and carts, stretching right down the road.

There was a white sheet hanging out of one of Herr Zimmer's windows. Another white sheet hung from the Archangel's house, fluttering in the wind.

My mother explained what they were for. "They're to show that people are surrendering," she said. "If you hang a white cloth from your window, that means surrender."

"Why are they surrendering?" I asked.

"Because they're afraid of the Russians."

"Why aren't *we* surrendering?"

"We haven't got any spare white sheets," said my mother.

This was untrue; Frau von Braun had a number of white sheets put away in a cupboard.

"Don't the Archangel and Herr Zimmer mind surrendering?" I asked.

My mother shrugged her shoulders. She said, "They're the sort who would always surrender. Seven years ago they surrendered to Hitler and the Nazis. Now they're surrendering to the Russians, and if some other set of people come along next year, they'll just surrender to them!"

"How many Russians are coming, then?" I asked. And then: "Can they speak German?" And: "Will they do anything to us?"

My mother was staring at the column of Russians and horses and carts, and did not answer. But suddenly she started in alarm. "Oh, my God!" she cried. "Christel—the uniform! Daddy's uniform! They mustn't find it, whatever happens! Quick, run! Get me the uniform—bring it to the kitchen!"

I ran to our bedroom, and lay down flat by my bed. The cardboard box containing the uniform was right underneath it, pushed against the wall. I pulled out the big brown box. There was a piece of string tied tightly round it, and I couldn't get the knots undone. I wrenched the string off the box; it cut my fingers. I removed the box lid and flung out the old newspapers on top, all copies of the *Völkischer Beobachter*. Underneath was the uniform, trousers and jacket, cap and leather belt. I snatched the things up, dropping the belt. The iron swastika buckle clinked.

I bent to pick up the belt, clutched the grey-green bundle of uniform to me, and ran across the room, into the next room, out of that room, into the salon.

Out in the street I could hear the noise of carts and horses and foreign voices. I could catch an occasional word quite clearly.

The sky outside the window was blue. Sunlight fell through the dirty window panes onto the parquet floor, the rolled-up carpet and the linen covers on the monster-armchairs. The door of the Uncles' Room was open, and some of the uncles were staring at me.

"Come on, Christel!" my mother called from the kitchen. "Oh, do hurry, please!"

My mother's voice sounded very quiet, and a very long way off, and suddenly the door into the hall seemed a very long way off too.

I stared at the roll of carpet at my feet. It was extraordinarily long. It was going to take me ages to reach the kitchen.

I walked slowly along the roll of carpet. Everything seemed as if I were seeing it through opera glasses the wrong way round, and the linen-covered chandelier was hanging askew. Particles of dust floated in the sunbeams. The pictures in the Uncles' Room suddenly grew to the size of wardrobes, shrank again to the size of playing cards, then swelled up to wardrobe-size once more.

I stood quite still, unable to move.

My mother appeared in the salon door. She was as small as a toy in a birdcage. She came towards me, growing larger all the time, growing enormous. She snatched the bundle of uniform from me and ran back to the kitchen. When she reached the salon door she went tiny again.

I don't know how long I stood there, staring at the uncles and the particles of dust, the chandelier and the roll of carpet. Suddenly there was a loud knock at the door of the house, and a deep voice shouted something in a language I did not understand.

I went through the salon towards the hall. The salon was back to its normal size. The uncles stared down at me; they were the right size too. The chandelier was hanging perfectly straight again.

I reached the kitchen door, and saw my mother standing by the stove, holding a poker and muttering, "Oh, for God's sake, for God's sake. . . ."

The stove was emitting clouds of smoke and a horrible smell. One leg of the uniform trousers was still hanging out of the open stove door. My mother was desperately trying to cram it in with the poker, but there was no room for it. I held my breath, counting the knocks at the front door. There were seventeen sets of three knocks each—after every burst of three the person on the other side of the door paused—and after those fifty-one knocks my father and Frau von Braun came up the cellar steps.

"We'll have to open the door, or they'll break it down," whispered Frau von Braun.

My mother saw my father standing in the hall, dropped the poker, ran to him and pushed him back to the cellar door. "Are you crazy?" she hissed. "Get back down to the cellar, quick! We can manage this without you. Do you want to get caught straight away? What good do you think that'll do anyone?"

My father hesitated. But Frau von Braun too made signs to him to go back down, and at last he nodded. My mother heaved a sigh of relief. In spite of the state of his legs, my father was young and strong, which was bound to strike any Russian as suspicious. All young, strong men were either dead or in the army these days, and it would make little difference to the Russians whether my father was still a German soldier, or whether he had stopped being a soldier a few weeks before. To the Russians, all German soldiers were enemies, and enemies must be taken prisoner and sent to Siberia.

My mother went back to the kitchen, closing the kitchen door after her.

Frau von Braun took a deep breath, tried to smile, and said to me, "Well then, here goes!" She went to the front door and pushed back the big brass bolt.

The door opened. I saw two men in yellowish-grey uniforms, each with a bright red five-pointed star on his uniform. One of the men was huge, with very broad shoulders, and the other was big too, but not so broad, and much younger. He was holding his cap in his hand—he had light brown crew-cut hair—and he was smiling.

The broad-shouldered man said something I did not understand. He walked into the hall, looked around, and said something else, which again I did not understand. He glanced at the cellar door, glanced at the salon, asked, "Soldier here? Not soldier?"

Frau von Braun shook her head. "Not soldier, not soldier, not, not!" she said firmly.

The broad-shouldered man opened the kitchen door. The kitchen was full of smoke, but the stove door was closed. My mother had taken the cast-iron hotplates off the top of the stove. They were lying round the floor, and a large, grey-green bundle with charred black spots on it stuck out of the stove top. Just as the broad-shouldered man came into the kitchen, my mother put the big kettle on top of the grey-green mound and pushed it down, hard. Then she turned round, red in the face and sweating. She looked at the big, broad-shouldered man and smiled. He smiled back, saying, "Not good, not good!"

He was pointing to the stove. He went to the window and opened it. He pointed first to the bright blue sky and the sun, then at the roof.

My mother nodded vigorously, making a great many gestures to convey what a nuisance it was when the sun shone straight down the chimney and made the stove smoke.

The shorter soldier, the one with the crew cut, was leaning in the kitchen doorway, coughing a bit because of the smoke. I went over and smiled up at him.

The soldier took hold of my long, brown pigtail and examined it. Then he narrowed his eyes, squinting, pursed his lips and went "Aaaaaaaah!" I giggled, feeling flattered. It was obvious that he thought I was pretty.

Gradually the smoke dispersed through the kitchen window. The tall, broad-shouldered soldier drank a glass of water.

My sister and Hildegard came up the cellar steps, and stopped in the cellar doorway. I beckoned them over. Still hesitating, they came into the kitchen.

"This all your child?" the broad-shouldered man asked my mother.

My mother shook her head. Hildegard went and stood beside Frau von Braun, who put her arm round Hildegard's shoulders. My sister stationed herself beside my mother, my mother put her arm round my sister's shoulders, I went over to join them, and her other arm went round my shoulders.

The broad-shouldered man seemed to like these family introductions. He nodded, and said, "Pretty child! Many pretty child!"

Then Gerald, evidently wishing to be thought a pretty child

too, came into the kitchen and went over to Frau von Braun to complete the family group.

At this, however, the broad-shouldered man's face darkened, and his eyes narrowed to small black slits. He had a large and stubbly jaw. He pointed to Gerald. *"Germanski, Germanski!"*

Gerald happened to be the only one of us who had blond hair and blue eyes and very fair skin.

Frau von Braun, wringing her hands, assured the Russian that her poor Gerald was not a *Germanski*, not a German. She swore it—he was a native Austrian, though, alas, a very blond one.

Up till now I had always wished *I* had fair hair and blue eyes. All the best-looking boys and girls in books and films, on posters or in the newspaper were blond and blue-eyed. Now I was glad I was so dark. However, I did not understand the bit about Austrians and *Germanski*. *Germanski* was what the Russians called German people; I got that all right. But what made us Austrians and not Germans all of a sudden? I'd been told at least once a day at school how Providence had chosen me to be a little German girl.

The broad-shouldered man went up to Gerald and looked closely at him, the way Herr Benedikt, who collected stamps, used to look at his stamp collection. He grasped Gerald's fair hair, felt the lobes of Gerald's ears, stroked Gerald's eyebrows. You could tell he was not at all happy about Gerald.

Gerald began to cry. Frau von Braun kept on talking to the broad-shouldered man, who did not understand her. He growled crossly.

The soldier with the crew cut was still standing in the kitchen doorway. I looked at him. He had stopped smiling, but he nodded to me. Then he went over to the broad-shouldered man, and they talked to each other. We could not understand a word of their conversation, but one thing was clear: the crew-cut man was on Gerald's side, and was trying to win the other one over. Apparently he succeeded. The broad-shouldered Russian stopped examining Gerald, took one last, suspicious glance around the kitchen, and then went out and left the house. The Russian with bristly hair said *"Da svidanya"* to us, and followed the broad-shouldered man. We stood perfectly still. We waited until both men had passed the kitchen window and disappeared round the corner of the house, and then I ran to the big window in the salon. The column of horses and carts and soldiers was still going along the street. I watched the broad-shouldered man and the man with the crew cut go through our garden gate, walk along the fence, and disappear through the gate of the Archangel's house. Angel, your hour has come! I thought. Your pretty hair ribbons won't do you much good now, Angel, because your hair is so fair. Nor your doll's pram either! That broad-shouldered man will kill you, and the other one with the crew-cut hair won't help you, because he's *my* friend, not yours! He won't put in a good word for *you*, Angel!

I hopped along the roll of carpet, all through the salon and into the kitchen. There was no one there but Gerald, who was standing by the kitchen table crying, beating his fists on the table-top and shouting over and over again, "The pigs! The brutes! The stupid pigs!"

"Where are the others?" I asked.

Gerald did not answer me. He went on crying and calling the Russians names. I thought the others would probably have gone down to the cellar to tell my father what had happened. I wondered whether to try and comfort Gerald, but I could not think of anything to say. His hair really was extremely blond, and his eyes terribly blue. And I'd never liked his fair skin much, either. I went down to the cellar.

Shooting the chandelier—My father is angry— I am angry—Legs like rotten plums

A great many more Russians walked into the house that day, and we left the door unbolted. They came in groups of three or four and marched through the house, opening cupboards, pulling out drawers, rolling up rugs, pulling the curtains open and shut by their tasselled cords—open and shut, open and shut, again and again—and looking inside the pans on the stove, which held nothing but beans and noodles.

They were all quite crazy about watches. I could not see why they wanted to collect so many. Each man had at least one on his wrist already, yet they kept asking, "Watch? Watch?" and seemed very sad when no watches were forthcoming.

They took other things too, but they did not seem to set any particular store by these, for we found a number of them in the garden afterwards. They had thrown them away almost as soon as they got outside the door.

I remember one Russian in particular, a man who came by himself; he was tall and strong, with a squint. I stood by the door as he came in, and greeted him politely. My mother had given me strict instructions to be polite to all the soldiers. I didn't mind. I smiled and said hello all afternoon, like a well-trained parrot. At first I said "Good afternoon" in German, but by now I was trying out some Russian phrases, saying, *"Da svidanya"* or *"Strastvitye,"* much to the delight of the soldiers.

The man I remember so well, however, did not smile or even return my greeting. He walked through the hall and into the salon, with me following him. He looked at the chandelier in its linen cover. He stared at it for some time, and then took out his pistol and fired at it. There was a loud bang, and a lot of dust and splinters of glass trickled out of two holes in the linen cover.

It was not my chandelier. It belonged to old Frau von Braun, who was horrible and had a hooked red nose, and wore a plush coat. I enjoyed watching the glass rain down. The Russian with the squint took another shot. This time he was aiming at the thick red cord from which the chandelier hung. His first shot hit the middle window of the salon. His next one got the glass-fronted cabinet with the porcelain shepherdesses. Finally he hit the red cord, and the linen-covered monster crashed to the floor. The cover came off. Splintered glass and crystal drops from the chandelier were all over the floor, mixed up with the electric light fittings, and coils of wire and bits of bent metal.

I would have liked to smile at the man with the squint and show him the other chandelier in the next room. But he was still holding his pistol, and I was not too sure whether he would see much difference between me and a chandelier. So I stayed safe behind the salon door, watching him pick his way over the broken glass.

I waited, hoping to hear more shots. I thought the chandelier in the Uncles' Room would crash onto the piano any moment now. But all was quiet. Then the man with the squint came back, crunching over the broken glass, passed me and went into the hall. He was carrying the uncle who was really Gerald and Hildegard's grandfather under one arm. When he got to the door I called out, *"Da svidanya! Strastvitye!"*

The Russian with the squint turned, still holding his pistol.

Oh, come on! I thought. Give us a smile, can't you? I'm not a chandelier. I haven't got fair hair, either. Come on, smile! My eyes are dark brown. Very dark.

The Russian with the squint did not smile, but he put his pistol away. He picked up the grandfather-uncle in both hands and went away.

I wanted to go into the salon and walk about on the broken glass, but my mother would not let me. She came and dragged me away, not down to the cellar this time, but up to the loft at the very top of the house, above the attic floor. My father had moved his quarters to this loft, which was felt to be safer.

I climbed the rickety ladder in front of my mother, and scrambled through the square trapdoor into the loft. The others were all sitting there, and they were furious with me. They had thought the shots they heard were aimed at *me*.

My father lost his temper and shouted at me, saying I was the stupidest child he'd ever known. "When a plane comes flying low you stand out in the open gawking at it!" he shouted. "When the Russians march in you stand at the garden gate chatting to that old fool Wawra, and when some crazy drunk of a Russian goes firing his pistol off around the place, you just stand there watching him!"

I felt very indignant, because I had not been gawking, and old Herr Wawra was not a fool, and the Russian with the squint was not crazy, and I shouted back, "I'm not stupid! You're the one who's stupid! You couldn't wait for the Russians to get here, so the war would be over and the Nazis would go away. And now the Russians *are* here, and the Nazis *have* gone away, and the war *is* over!"

My father did not answer.

I was still so furious that I went on, "*I* haven't been in Russia! *I* wasn't ever a German soldier! *I* haven't shot any Russians dead; I haven't, so *I* don't have to hide up in lofts! I don't have to hide! I don't have to hide!"

My mother made a move towards me, but it was very

cramped in the loft, and in order to slap me she would have had to climb over Hildegard and Gerald first. And my father said, "Leave her alone! Don't hit her. She's right, after all. She's quite right."

I huddled in the farthest corner of the loft, making out that I was hurt. I was not really hurt, just pretending; in actual fact I was ashamed of myself for saying that to my father, about killing Russians. It had not been nice of me. I shut my eyes.

The others were arguing as to where my father would be safest: up in the loft or down in the cellar?

My father said he would not be safe anywhere, and he was sick of hiding in any case. He said he would simply let the Russians see him around the place, the same as us, and pretend that he was an invalid who had been unable to join the army because of his bad legs.

"Suppose they don't believe you?" said my mother.

My father had no answer to that, but he did come down from the loft, limped out of the house, leaning on a stick, and sat down by the stream in the meadow, beside the garden gnomes.

"The man must be out of his mind," groaned Frau von Braun.

My mother got a broom and swept up the broken glass in the salon, cutting her fingers several times. "He *is* out of his mind," she agreed.

However, he was not out of his mind at all; he turned out to be quite right. Next morning some of the Russian soldiers came back. They had to find a billet for their major, and they liked the look of our house, despite the absence of one chandelier. An hour later the Major moved in, along with a number of other soldiers, and we could never have kept my father hidden from them for long. On their first meeting the Major looked suspiciously at my father, and kept saying, "You young! You soldier! You was soldier!" Then my father showed the Major his bad legs, rolling up the legs of his trousers and unwrapping the old teacloths he was using for bandages. His legs looked dreadful. By now it was impossible to tell whether they had been wounded by Russian shells or were the result of tuberculosis of the bone, or leprosy, or what. There were huge red sores on them, each with a small yellow hole in it, full of pus, and the skin between these sores was dark blue and shiny. My father's legs looked like rotten plums.

The Major and his soldiers were satisfied, and believed my father. The Major even gave him a box of muslin bandages and a packet of powder to put on his legs, and a soldier brought him a little bag full of some kind of strange-smelling tea for bathing them.

The kitchen in the summerhouse—The cook— An ugly, smelly, crazy, little man— The city of Leningrad

My mother and Frau von Braun were delighted about the Major. Apparently it was a very good thing to have a major in the house, because of the man who shot the chandelier, and the man who stole the picture of the uncle, and the one who was so suspicious of Gerald, and the ones who wanted watches.

"The private soldiers will take care to leave the Major's house alone," my mother explained.

And the Major really did turn out to be a good catch. Not only was he very polite and very clean and very handsome but he also had tobacco, and he gave some to my father, which was a stroke of luck for us, because when my father had to go without tobacco he would get very irascible and fierce, almost as fierce as Grandmother.

The Major commandeered Frau von Braun's bedroom. There was always a young soldier standing outside the door between the bedroom and the salon, doing something or other to the Major's uniform—either cleaning the Major's boots, or brushing the Major's jacket, or polishing the Major's coat buttons. Sometimes he sat cross-legged outside the bedroom door, darning the Major's socks. The Major's socks were black, and the Major got very annoyed if this orderly who looked after his uniform darned his black socks with brown wool. "Heavens above, how vain that man is!" said Frau von Braun. "Talk about peacocks!"

As soon as the Major had moved in and inspected my father, he inspected the garden. He asked for the key to the bigger summerhouse, looked the place over, and decided that it would do for a cookhouse.

Soon afterwards, a horse and cart drove into our garden, right through the rose bed. Frau von Braun groaned; she had been looking forward to the first roses. There was an enormous iron pot and a big black stove on the cart, and in front, in the driver's seat, sat a very strange figure.

Hildegard and my sister giggled behind their hands, and Gerald grinned. "Good gracious me, what an ugly little gnome of a man!" said Frau von Braun.

The man driving the cart was very small, with a stomach as round as a ball, a shiny bald head, thin arms, bow legs, and curly black tufts of hair behind his ears, which stuck out. He wore old-fashioned metal-framed glasses. He had very few teeth, and those he did have were bad. His skin was sallow and greasy. He wore a uniform coat, but somehow it did not look like part of a uniform. This odd little driver brought his vehicle to a halt right by the summerhouse, in the middle of the snowdrop bed. He climbed down from the cart, looked around him, looked at us and gave us a shy, timid, wry smile.

He was very close to me. His coat and trousers, made of some kind of coarse-woven material, had little spots of dirt on them, and he smelled of vegetable soup and bacon and tobacco and sweat. He smelled of other things besides. He smelled foreign; it was a nice, friendly foreign smell. As he looked at me his round glasses wobbled on his hooked nose.

I said, "*Da svidanya*, comrade!"

He nodded, and winked one eye, one tiny little, round, light grey eye, which now became a tiny little, light grey slit. He said to me, "How you do, missus?" And to the others he announced, "I going be cook here!" Then he made a bow, or something like it.

Afterwards, my sister said the cook was the ugliest person she had ever seen. And Hildegard said he was the smelliest person she had ever smelt. And my mother said he was the craziest person she had ever heard.

But to me he was the first ugly, smelly, crazy person I had ever loved. I would often sit beside the Russian cook; I liked being with him, even if the others did think it was silly of me. I loved the cook because there was absolutely nothing about him that had anything to do with war. He was a soldier, but he had no gun or pistol. He did have a uniform, but it looked more like a rag-and-bone man's outfit. He was a Russian, but he could speak German. He was an enemy, but he had a soft, deep voice for singing lullabies. His name was Cohn, and he came from Leningrad, where he had been a tailor. Cohn told me a lot of things, and when he finished he would always say, "Not matter, not matter, missus!"

"I am good tailor," he told me, "but never did make new trousers, new jackets. Always mending, only mending! People not have money. Not matter, not matter, missus!"

Another time he told me, "I know pretty woman. Is long time ago; was in Leningrad. She be married to other man by now. Not matter, not matter, missus!"

He told me a great deal about Leningrad. Leningrad was very far away, but Cohn made it seem quite close, so that I felt I really knew my way around the city. I knew the woman with the green head-scarf, where Cohn went to buy potatoes, and the man who got Cohn to sew a different button on his coat every week, the house where Cohn had his tailor's workshop in the cellar and the back wall by the ironing board was all damp. I got to know the family he did mending for with two sons studying medicine at the University, and the family that always had a huge dish of fried fish once a week. And I knew the way Cohn's aunt, a fat lady with two warts on her nose, smoked a goose; she did not actually smoke it, but hung it in the top of the roof to dry.

I felt as though I knew Leningrad inside out, but there I was wrong, as I realised only later. All I knew was Cohn's Leningrad, which was a tiny fragment of the whole gigantic city.

Mould—My father gets drunk—
The Angel's grandmother

Every day at our midday meal we had beef broth made from the little grey objects, boiled noodles with dehydrated onion, and bean salad without any vinegar in the dressing. When I complained my mother was cross and said, "You should be grateful to have anything to eat at all. Other people are starving!"

I was not grateful, however, because I knew perfectly well that there were still lots of jars of venison and fruit preserves, green beans and liver sausage in our hiding place down in the cellar. My mother and Frau von Braun guarded these jars jealously, much to the disgust of myself and Gerald. After all, we'd stolen them! We had more right to them than anyone else, and the grown-ups ought not to walk off with our jars like that! They did, though.

Gerald discovered the only way of getting at some of the venison *à la jardinière,* or the goulash, 1944. He would occasionally slip down to our secret store of provisions in the cellar, get one of the preserving jars and give the flap of the rubber ring between jar and lid a little tug. This let a tiny amount of air into the jar, and two or three days later you could see the faintest shimmer of pale green mould beginning to form on top of the brown gravy.

My mother went down to the cellar every day and inspected the food by the light of a candle, to make sure no mice were getting at the bags of beans and noodles and peas. If, in the course of this inspection, she came upon a jar of venison going mouldy on top, or one of apricots with green spots, she would sadly bring the jar upstairs. "Another jar about to go off," she mourned. "It's too damp down in that cellar."

We sympathised and said what a pity it was, winking at each other while my mother carefully scraped the mould off the gravy, with Frau von Braun watching anxiously to make sure she did not scrape away too much, or waste a scrap of the precious food.

"Oh, do go carefully!" said Frau von Braun, and we could see her swallow, because her mouth was watering with greed. "Oh, please—a little bit of mould won't hurt us!"

However, venison days were rare—a very occasional break in the monotony of the mounds of noodles with onions and oil.

It was a long time since the first two Russians had knocked their seventeen bursts of three knocks at our front door. The house was full of Russians now. There was Cohn in his kitchen in the summerhouse. The Major was billeted in Frau von Braun's bedroom. His orderly had the room next door, sharing it with another soldier, a red-haired man with a pimply face. There was a whole contingent of military police on the first floor, six or seven of them, including three women police officers, fat women with big buns of hair and black wool stockings. One of them was called Ludmilla. She had holes in her stockings, and one big toe was always sticking out. Ludmilla was not at all friendly, and I avoided her.

A sergeant with a great many medals slept in the library. When he was drunk he sang at the top of his voice, but he stopped singing if the Major's orderly banged on his door. Besides all these people, soldiers billeted in the other villas nearby would visit our house, coming and going as they pleased.

My father had given up worrying about me; he had plenty of worries of his own, and besides, he was permanently drunk. This was not his fault; he was forced to drink all day and half the night. It had happened like this: The Russians, as I said earlier, were mad about watches, and in peacetime my father was a watchmaker. One of the military policemen, whose name was Ivan, brought my father tools for repairing watches: a swivel chair, pincers, tweezers, screwdrivers, magnifying glasses, files. He even found and brought along a big, bright carbide lamp and a real watchmaker's workbench.

My father put the workbench under the window of our room —we had only one room for ourselves now—and hung the carbide lamp from the crossbar of the window. He spent nearly all his time sitting there behind a great pile of watches. Russians would come into the room, clap him on the shoulder, fling their watches down on the bench, rummage around in the pile of watches until they found something that took their fancy, and pocket it. My father had stopped protesting. He tried to keep his various customers' watches separate on the first day, but he soon realised that they could not tell their watches apart themselves.

My father sat hunched over his work, his magnifying glass screwed into his right eye, looking up only when a customer clapped him on the shoulder, held out a bottle, and insisted, "Drink, comrade! You good comrade! Drink!" And like a good comrade, he drank . . . like a good comrade, he drank everything —apricot brandy, red wine, cognac, vermouth, pear liqueur, slivovitz. Sometimes you could see him swaying about on his swivel chair like a good comrade. Sometimes a watch would fall off the bench, and like a good comrade he would mutter: "Hell!" and I would pick it up for him. I liked my father when he was drunk.

As for my mother, she said, "Better to have *him* putting it away than the Russians!" My mother was afraid of the Russians when they were drunk; terrible tales were told about the things drunken Russians did. Perhaps they were true, perhaps not; who could tell? Not my mother.

The Archangel herself was a very odd sight these days. Her face was smeared with soot, and she wore floor-length woollen skirts, a ragged cardigan, a black wool head-scarf and a grey crochet shawl. With so many layers of clothes on, the Archangel could not flutter about any more; she crawled through the garden like a fat black beetle. The soldiers called the Archangel *Mamitchku* and tapped their foreheads behind her back. They thought she was a crazy old woman.

One day I met the Angel by the garden fence. I was pleased to see that she was no longer all dolled up with hair ribbons and a frilly dress. "Why does your mama go about in those silly clothes, looking so daft and funny?" I asked.

The Angel rocked back and forth on tip-toe, twiddled one blond curl round her forefinger, and said, "I don't have any mama. I never did have any mama. I've only got old Granny."

I stared at her, speechless.

The Angel leaned towards me, her mouth touching the wire of the fence. "I'll tell you, if you promise not to tell anyone else," she whispered.

I promised without hesitation. The Angel made me swear an oath, and then explained, "Mama has disguised herself so the Russians won't cut her breasts off!"

I leaned towards the fence in my turn, and whispered back, "Oh, but the Russians do much worse things to old ladies! They cut old ladies up and pickle them!"

The Angel ran away.

May Day—Loud singing—Soft singing—Our find

Once a day I crawled through the hole in the fence into Herr Wawra's garden, and slipped across to his summerhouse. Through the dirty little window I watched old Herr Wawra sitting on a rickety basket chair, sorting out his mixed stores of food. Day after day he sorted them, from morning till evening. He already had a large bag full of beans, and one of rather sugary noodles. I would have enjoyed talking to old Herr Wawra, but he did not like me any more; he did not like anyone any more, least of all the Russians, since they had not, after all, brought old Herr Goldmann back for him.

Old Herr Wawra slept in the summerhouse too these days, and sometimes he could be seen standing outside the summerhouse door, shaking his fist at the villa and cursing. He never used to swear before. There were thirty or forty Russians billeted in that villa, and they often sang songs in the evening. Their voices were loud and wild, but never out of tune. They were drunk. When we heard the Russians in Herr Wawra's villa singing their loud, wild songs my mother would not let me leave the house, though of course I went out all the same.

One evening the Russians in Herr Wawra's house were singing particularly loud, and the Russians in the Archangel's house were singing too, celebrating the first of May. Our Major was not at home; he had gone to some May Day festivities at the Russians' local H.Q. When the Major was out my mother and Frau von Braun were nervous and edgy. I was sitting on my bed in our room, with my sister lying beside me reading a book called *The Easter Hare's School*. *The Easter Hare's School* was the only children's book we had found among all the thick, leather-bound books in the library. By now I knew the story by heart, and of course my sister did too, but all the same I snatched the book from her, shouting that it was mine, slammed it shut and sat on it.

My sister was delighted to accept my challenge; she was bored too. She boxed my ears. I pulled her pigtails. My father shouted at us, inquiring whether, for God's sake, he couldn't have a bit of peace now it was May Day and the Russians were celebrating, and he didn't have to repair watches for once? He was shouting because he was out of cigarettes; he had an enormous box of tobacco, but no cigarette papers left. He tried putting the cigarette tobacco into a pipe, but he did not really enjoy it that way.

I gave my sister one last little kick, got off the bed, and went over to the door.

"Where are you going?" asked my mother. She was standing in front of a bowl of warm water, trying to wash some under-clothes without any soap or detergent.

"To the lavatory," I said. This was my standard excuse when I wanted to make a getaway. I closed the door of our room behind me, and went to the front door. On my way I passed the kitchen, where I saw Frau von Braun, and also, unexpectedly, the Angel and the Archangel, bundled up in her old clothes. The Archangel was announcing, "Frau von Braun, I simply *must* stay here, even if it means sleeping on the floor! They're worse than ever today! They're celebrating May Day by getting drunk!"

The front door was locked, and though the key was on the inside of the door it squealed when you turned it. So I slipped into the salon, passing the kitchen door again, and heard the Archangel going on, "They've got a whole barrel of red wine in the house, and three big jugs of vodka! Dear Frau von Braun, I beg you to let me shelter here! After all, your house is under the Major's protection, and the Major is a fine man, an educated man, he won't allow any atrocities!"

I climbed out of the middle window of the salon and jumped out into the ivy. I leaned against the wall, listening to the singing from Herr Wawra's villa and the shouting from the Archangel's house. Sometimes it sounded very loud, and then it would go quite soft again, because of the wind. The wall against which I was leaning was cold. I looked up to the sky in search of stars. I saw one; I thought it was Venus. I remembered that Venus is the evening star and the morning star, as Grandfather had told me. I thought of Grandfather. The wall against which I was leaning became even colder. I had not thought of Grandfather for weeks. I couldn't understand how I could *not* have thought of him. The man had come in the plane, the man with the brown leather cap, and Grandfather had gone home to his Juli, to Grandmother. He would have got to the Alszeile, or somewhere around there, when I went off to the NSV Home in search of noodles and stopped thinking about Grandfather. Could a person actually die because you stopped thinking about him?

I went to visit Cohn, who was sitting in his summerhouse kitchen in his long grey underpants and a long-sleeved grey vest, reading a piece of newspaper by candlelight. He put the paper down when I opened the summerhouse door. "Good evening, missus," he said, standing up. He went over to the cupboard and found a piece of sausage. "You like, missus?"

I shook my head. The sausage had too many lumps of fat in it.

"You not like? Not matter!" said Cohn, returning the sausage to the cupboard. He listened to the singing and the shouting. "Much drinking, much singing, not good, not good," he said, troubled.

I said, "Not matter, not matter!"

Cohn sat down at the table again, balanced his glasses on the end of his nose, pushed them back up again, and explained, "Good man, he drinks, turns into bad man. Not know what he does."

I looked at Cohn's newspaper. Not only was the language foreign, even the letters were unfamiliar. I pointed to a line in very big, black type. "What does that say, Cohn?"

"That says, war soon over," said Cohn.

"But the war *is* over!" I cried.

"Is over here," Cohn told me. "Is not yet over in all Germany. Nazis still fighting. Still shooting!" He tore a scrap of paper off the sheet of newspaper, rolled it into a little tube and filled it with the crumbly black tobacco called *machorka*. Cohn picked up the candle and lit his *machorka* cigarette.

"If the war is soon over," I asked, "will you all be going back to Russia again?"

Cohn nodded.

"Are you glad?"

Cohn's tiny little eyes looked at me through his thick lenses. He shrugged his shoulders. The *machorka* cigarette was stuck between the gap in his bottom teeth.

"Are you glad?" I asked again.

"Not home for five years," murmured Cohn. "Will be much different. Much, much quite different!"

"Why aren't you with the rest of them?" I pointed in the direction of Herr Wawra's villa and the May Day festivities. "Why aren't you singing and shouting and drinking?"

Cohn pushed the *machorka* cigarette stub out of the gap in his teeth with his thick red tongue. It fell on the ground, glowed briefly, and went out. Cohn sighed. "I not drink. I not shout."

"But you can sing, can't you?"

Cohn smiled. And then he sang for me. He sang in a soft, deep voice, a voice for singing lullabies. The words he sang were not Russian. I could have sat like that for a long, long time listening to Cohn singing. Perhaps I did sit there for a long, long time listening to him singing.

I don't remember now, but in any event, the summerhouse door suddenly opened and Gerald came in. "Hey, Christel," Gerald said. "Your mother's having fits! She's been looking for you all over the house!"

"So what? Let her look!" I shouted.

"Come on," Gerald insisted. "It's after eleven!"

Cohn had stopped singing and was rolling himself another cigarette. "Oh, missus, missus!" he said. "Must do what mama says!"

I got up, muttering rebelliously, and followed Gerald out of the summerhouse-kitchen.

"Why are you always chasing off to see that horrid little gnome?" asked Gerald.

"Horrid little gnome yourself!"

"Did you know the Archangel has gone and landed herself and the Angel on us because they're afraid of the Russians?"

"I've known that for ages!"

There was still a glimmer of light from the kitchen, but the other windows were darkened.

We went towards the big, black square of the house and the small, bright square of the kitchen window. There was something large and dark lying in the ivy outside the kitchen window, snoring. It was our much-decorated sergeant. The sergeant was not a friend of mine. He had cold eyes and thin, compressed lips. He looked dangerous. But now here he was with his mouth open, snoring, and his eyes closed, and he had no idea that I was standing there looking down at him with a grin. There was a strong smell of brandy about him.

I enjoyed seeing him helpless like that. I wished I had a torch so as to see him better. I would have liked to spit into his open mouth, too, but I was afraid that might wake him up.

Gerald came and pulled my sleeve. "Come over here," he said in an excited whisper. "I've got something to show you! I found it! Come on!"

He dragged me away from the square of light and the sergeant. He was holding something. "I nearly fell over this," he said. "It was lying beside him. He's drunk!" Gerald had the sergeant's pistol.

"Oh, well done!" I whispered, excited myself. "What shall we do with it? We'll have to hide it!"

"Where?"

"In the ivy."

"No, that's no good," said Gerald. "I'm not going near that sergeant again—he's horrible, and I bet he'd wake up."

"Well, how about the garden gnome's wheelbarrow, then?"

Gerald agreed to this idea, and we went off to the meadow behind the house. It was quite dark now, and we were some time finding the garden gnome with the wheelbarrow. It turned out he had fallen over, but we stood him up again, and Gerald put the pistol in his wheelbarrow. I pulled up some tufts of grass and covered the pistol with them, and then we slipped back home and climbed in through the middle window of the salon. Something moved by the door of the Uncles' Room; there was someone standing there. It gave me a nasty fright. However, there was nothing to be frightened of. It was only my mother standing there, and she was too tired even to scold me much.

A short night—The empty bed—Afraid—
The sub-machine gun—The sergeant—
The sergeant's medals

Though it must have been well past midnight, I could not
get to sleep. Close to me—very close to me, because she kept
moving closer in the night—my sister was grinding her teeth in
her sleep, and sometimes clicking her tongue as well. Behind me,
my father was tossing and turning in bed, making the bed creak.
My father grunted; my mother was snoring rather loudly. The
sound of the Russian festivities came in through the closed
window; I could no longer tell if the noise came from Herr
Wawra's house or the Archangel's. I put my thumb in my mouth.
My thumb tasted of grass and earth, and I remembered the tufts
of grass I had pulled up, and the sergeant's pistol. I sucked my
thumb; it tasted bitter. I decided I was going to start up a gang
—a gang with a real pistol! I worked the earth out from under
my thumbnail with my teeth, and swallowed it. Then I curled
my feet up and rubbed between my toes with my forefingers.
While comfortably occupied like this I fell asleep.

I woke, opened my eyes, and realised it was not quite light
yet. I closed my eyes again, turned over on my front and tried to
get back to sleep, to recapture a bit of my pleasant dream again.
But I could hear noises. Were the Russians still celebrating May
Day? Wasn't that the Archangel's high-pitched voice squawking
away? I sat up in bed and looked around me. My mother and
father's big bed was empty. They were gone. My sister was sitting
huddled in her bed, the blanket wrapped round her shoulders,
looking at me with scared eyes.

"What's up?" I asked.

My sister went on staring. She had stuck four fingers in her
mouth and was nibbling at them. I crept over to my sister's bed,

went right up close to her, and asked her again what was happening. My sister was not too sure. She said there had been some soldiers in the room when she woke up, angry soldiers, with a gun, and they had made Mummy and Daddy get out of bed.

"Where did they take them?"

My sister did not know. I groped around for my dress, and found it lying beside the bed.

"Where are you going?" asked my sister.

"To find out what's happening," I said. "That noise is in the kitchen." I put my dress on, realised that it was inside out with the seams showing, and decided I didn't mind. It was an ugly dress anyway.

"I daren't go!" my sister whispered.

"I daren't stay here!" I told her.

My sister put her clothes on too, and we crept barefoot out of the room, across the salon, and up to the kitchen door. We were trembling, not just from fright, for it was quite cold so early in the morning. The kitchen door was closed, but now I could clearly hear the Archangel's wails inside the kitchen. "Mercy, mercy, please!" she was wailing.

However, I could also hear a Russian voice, much louder than the Archangel's. The Russian voice sounded very angry. I bent down to look through the keyhole, but all I could see was a patch of yellowish grey. Sometimes the yellowish-grey patch was quite close to the keyhole, and then it would move a little further off. I realised there was someone in a Russian uniform on the other side of the door. I did not really want to go into that kitchen, but all the same I suddenly found myself there, right in the middle of the room, with my sister stumbling in after me. I am still not sure just how I did get in; either I must have grasped the door handle as I was peering through the keyhole and opened the door by mistake, or the soldier on the other side heard me and my sister and opened it himself.

I stood there quite unable to move; I could never move at all when I was extremely frightened. I was staring at the sub-machine gun in front of me, held by the much-decorated sergeant. He was sitting at the kitchen table staring at me, and there was a bottle of wine on the table.

The sub-machine gun was actually swaying back and forth, but to me it looked perfectly steady; indeed, it seemed the only thing in the kitchen that *was* steady. Everything else was going round and round, circling around the sub-machine gun. They were all going round in circles: the sergeant, the stove, the two soldiers at the door, the kitchen table, the wine bottle on the table, the window, and the pale blue tiles of the wall where all the others were standing—my father, Frau von Braun, my sister too, Hildegard, the Archangel, the Angel, Gerald. I could hear every word being spoken or shouted or whispered in the kitchen with perfect clarity.

"Come over here. Come and stand beside us," said my father.

"We're under the Major's protection!" wailed the Archangel.

"What does he want?" asked Hildegard, beginning to cry.

And the sergeant kept on shouting, "Gone! All **gone**! You gone! You gone! All gone!"

I felt a hand on the nape of my neck—a horny, calloused hand like a cheese grater. I leaned back, resting my whole weight against this hand.

The owner of the hand said quietly in my ear, "You come. Stand with mama. Not shout, keep quiet, not cry."

I recognised his voice. It was the voice of the Major's orderly and I knew it very well, because we often played a word game together. He would say, *"Tschto eto taboye?"* and I would put it into German: "What is that?" He said, *"Eta krovaty,"* and I said, "That is a bed." He said, *"Eta kniga,"* and I said, "That is a book." He said, *"Eta vedra,"* and I said, "That is a bucket."

The familiar hand and voice led me over to the wall with the pale blue tiles, and placed me beside my mother. My mother laid a hand on my shoulder. The sergeant did not seem to like this move, for he turned the sub-machine gun to point at my mother, and she took her hand away. Watching the sub-machine gun all the time, she said quietly, "The fool lost his pistol when he was drunk. He thinks we've stolen it."

"It's in the garden gnome's wheelbarrow," I said, looking straight into the gun.

Apparently I had not spoken loud enough, for my mother just went on staring ahead of her. The sergeant put the sub-machine gun down on his lap, across his knees, reached for the bottle of wine, drank and drank and drank. I wished he would go on drinking for ever and never stop. I could breathe more easily when the gun was down on the sergeant's knees, and the sergeant's eyes were closed, and the bottle was in his mouth.

"It's in the garden gnome's wheelbarrow," I told my mother again.

"Be quiet!" whispered my mother.

"But it *is!* Gerald and I . . ."

"Be quiet, will you?"

I did not understand. We could so easily have got the pistol and given it back to the drunken sergeant, and then surely he would leave us all alone! Why wouldn't my mother understand? I would have to tell my father. He was standing beside my mother against the wall, and anyway I'd rather stand next to my father. I wriggled behind my mother and pushed myself between her and my father.

The sergeant noticed a movement by the wall as he drank. He put the bottle down, picked up his sub-machine gun, and shouted again. He was very drunk indeed. It was not just the gun swaying; the sergeant was swaying too. He and his sub-machine gun even swayed round in the direction of the door where the two soldiers were standing guard, and the soldiers ducked in alarm.

"His pistol is in the garden gnome's wheelbarrow," I told my father.

My father too said, "Be quiet."

"But suppose I go and fetch it?"

"Then he'll shoot you. He's bent on shooting whoever took his pistol."

Would the sergeant really shoot me? I looked at his face, though I found it difficult to keep my eyes on his face and not his sub-machine gun. The sergeant did not have a real face any more. He had hair, eyes, a mouth, a nose, a stubbly chin and sticking-out ears, but it did not add up to a face. None of it seemed to fit; it crumpled into little bits and disintegrated, and could not be put back together. A face like that told you nothing. I thought better of going to fetch the pistol.

The sergeant had another drink, and put the sub-machine gun down on the table. Then he put the bottle down too and began to cry. Tears ran down his stubbly cheeks to his chin, and somehow they put his ruined, crumbling face together again. The sergeant had his face back. The sergeant was sobbing. I did not understand what he was saying, except for one word: he kept on and on repeating, "Stalin . . . Stalin . . . Stalin."

At this point the sergeant began tearing the medals off his

chest. He stopped shouting words now; he was weeping bitterly, and his medals were lying about the floor and the table. One dangled from the top of his boot. The Major's orderly, standing by the kitchen door, whispered something in an urgent tone to the other soldier.

My father sighed. "Oh, bloody hell!" he said. He walked slowly towards the sergeant. It was only three steps to the table, but those three steps took a very long time. My mother gripped my shoulder, holding me very tight. Her fingers dug in below my collar bone, leaving four blue marks that lasted for weeks. I prayed to the sergeant. I felt that the sergeant was like God. My father managed to take those three steps. God was pointing the sub-machine gun straight at his stomach, but God did not shoot. Very, very slowly my father hitched a kitchen chair towards him with his foot. He began talking to the sergeant in Russian, very quietly. In among the foreign words I kept hearing him say, "Stalin . . . Stalin . . . Stalin" over and over again.

God the Sergeant lowered the sub-machine gun, put it down between his legs. My father lowered himself onto the kitchen chair, still talking, never stopping for a moment. He bent down, still talking, picked up a medal, talked and talked, put the medal back on the sergeant's chest. The sergeant swayed again, made a wild gesture, tried to tear the medal off once more, could not manage it, and allowed my father to replace another medal, and then another.

Carefully, my father put the medals back on the sergeant's chest, the way one hangs fragile glass bells and shiny ornaments on a Christmas tree. When all the medals were back in place—except for one, which was lying under the table, out of sight of both the sergeant and my father—the sergeant put his head down on my father's shoulder, mumbled, "Comrade, comrade . . ." and fell fast asleep.

Supporting the sergeant with one hand, so that he would not slip from his shoulder and off the chair, my father drew the sub-machine gun out from between his legs with his other hand. The sergeant twitched and muttered something, but he did not wake up.

However, the Major's orderly, over by the door, growled suspiciously. The sight of my father holding the sub-machine gun worried him. Guns belonged in Russian hands. My father offered the sub-machine gun to the Major's orderly, who came slowly closer, took hold of it, and snatched it away. He was still growling, but he was not really angry; it was just that he was not sure what to do. In actual fact he was rather grateful to my father for calming the sergeant down, but my father had spoken so much fluent Russian that the orderly could hardly help realising this was a German soldier who must have spent some years in Russia. Maybe even in the orderly's own village, where there was nothing left now but a few mud huts in ruins.

The Major's orderly gave my father a long, steady look. Then he glanced at the other soldier by the door. The other soldier nodded. The Major's orderly nodded too, and suddenly grinned and told my father, "You are a friend!" I had taught him this phrase only the day before, when we were playing the dictionary game.

My father pointed to the sub-machine gun and said something in Russian. The orderly hesitated, but the soldier by the door cried, "Da, da!" which means, "Yes, yes!" So then the orderly said, "Da da!" too, and took the ammunition out of the gun. He put it in his trouser pocket, and propped the empty sub-machine gun up against the kitchen table. Then he pulled the sergeant out of the kitchen chair and set him on his feet. The sergeant seemed not to have a bone in his body; he collapsed into a yellowish-grey heap.

"Shit!" muttered the Major's orderly. This was not one of the words I had taught him; he knew it already.

The orderly took the limp and boneless sergeant's arms, and the other soldier came over from the door and took the limp and boneless sergeant's legs, and between them they picked him up. My father placed the sub-machine gun on his bemedalled chest, and the two soldiers carried him off to his bed in the library.

My father sighed, and wiped his forehead and throat with a handkerchief. When he took the handkerchief away it was damp. "I think I'm going to bed too," said my father. "And a very good morning to you all, ladies and gentlemen." He limped out of the kitchen door.

My living father—Gerald's dead father—
A garden party

My mother's fingers were still digging into me below my collar bone; it was only now that I noticed how much they hurt. It was some time before all of us standing there by the pale blue tiles of the wall could absorb the fact that the danger was past. Frau von Braun hesitated before she took a step away from the wall, and the Archangel began to sob, though cautiously.

At last my mother let go of my shoulder. "Get me a chair, or I shall fall," she said. "I feel dizzy!"

My sister got her a chair. She was trembling.

"But where *is* the sergeant's pistol?" asked Hildegard.

I could have hit her. Of all the silly questions!

"In the garden gnome's wheelbarrow," said my mother, sinking into the chair.

"What? How do you know?" asked the Archangel and Frau von Braun simultaneously.

My mother did not reply. I expect she was feeling sick; she always felt sick at moments of great stress.

Frau von Braun persisted. "Who put it in the wheelbarrow?"

Still my mother said nothing, but she looked first at me, then at Gerald, with a wealth of meaning in her glance. Frau von Braun understood. So did the Archangel.

"Oh, but that's—that's . . ." cried Frau von Braun. She did not seem to know just what "that" was, but she added, "Gerald! Gerald, come here at once!"

As for the Archangel, she screeched, "I always said so! That precious pair—little demons, demons in human shape, that's what *they* are! Risking all our lives! Did you ever hear of such a thing? What a way to behave! All our lives in danger, just because of those two little demons!"

Gerald dashed across the kitchen, ducking past Frau von Braun, who made a grab for him, and jumped out of the open window. I followed suit. We plunged through the ivy, and ran over the meadow to Cohn's kitchen in the summerhouse. We would be safe there.

Panting for breath, Gerald gasped, "The Angel was so frightened she went in her knickers! She was standing next to me by the wall. She stank like anything!"

I giggled.

"Were you frightened?" asked Gerald.

"Of course not," I said indignantly, adding, "I knew all along my father would make it all right. He's not afraid of anyone, certainly not that stupid old sergeant!"

Gerald nodded agreement.

I knew what a lie I was telling, and I looked hard at Gerald to see if he knew too.

The summerhouse door was still closed, and we sat down on the step outside. It was a stone step with a crack across it, and blades of grass growing in the crack. Gerald pulled up a blade of grass. "*My* father was never afraid of anything either," he said. "Not ever in his life. He always got into his plane laughing—he was pleased to be going up. He said it was a really wonderful feeling."

I wanted to change the subject. I did not like this talk of dead fathers. "Cohn's still asleep," I said. "Shall we knock and wake him up?"

Gerald was not interested in Cohn. "My father might still come back," he told me. "Those planes, you know, when they catch fire and crash you don't actually find the plane at all, just sort of bits and pieces. So suppose it was all a mistake, and my father didn't go up that day, and someone else went instead of him, then that person would be dead now and my father . . . ."

This was the silliest thing I had heard for a long time, and I interrupted Gerald. "If that happened your father would have written to say he was alive and well!"

"Oh, but he can't write, he was shot down over England, and the English would take a German prisoner at once, so he couldn't write."

"Listen, first you say perhaps he didn't fly that day at all, and someone else went instead, and then you say he *did* fly and now he's a prisoner in England. So which do you mean?"

Gerald shrugged his shoulders. "But he can't be just gone!" he muttered.

I remembered Schurli Berger from our old building. In spite of the official notification of death, he would not believe his father was dead, however often I explained it to him. There was nothing one could do. "Well, it could be like that," I said. "Maybe your father joined the underground and now he's fighting the last of the Nazis!"

Gerald liked this idea, and readily agreed to it. He promised that later, when his father came back from working with the resistance movement, he would give an enormous garden party, with all sorts of cream cakes and plenty of buns and raspberry-ade, and they would invite at least a hundred children, and there would be Japanese lanterns hanging in all the trees, and as the star attraction Gerald's father would do cartwheels all across the meadow.

"And where will your father get all those cream cakes and Japanese lanterns and raspberryade?" I inquired.

"Oh, that'll be easy," said Gerald. "Papa has important friends. The *Gauleiter* of Salzburg is a friend of his! And Granny, she's Papa's mother, she even knows Göring! She knows all the top Party members! We'll be able to get plenty of lanterns all right!"

I stood up and knocked on the summerhouse door to wake Cohn; I was sick and tired of talking about Gerald's dead father. This was really going too far: a resistance fighter who was friends with a *Gauleiter* and would get Japanese lanterns from Göring! "I'm going to see Cohn now," I told Gerald. "What are *you* going to do?"

Realising that I had had enough of his company, Gerald pulled up a few more blades of grass, put one of them in his mouth, got up and strolled slowly back to the house.

Cohn had woken up at last. He opened the summerhouse door, looking sleepy, and sniffed the fresh air. Then he saw me and brightened.

"Come on, missus, come on, is time! Time to cook, soldiers wanting breakfast."

"They won't be wanting any breakfast today!" I told him. "They're sleeping it off, after last night. I don't expect they'll wake up till midday."

Cohn shook his head. "Still, must go cook."

Not a single soldier came to the kitchen in the summerhouse for his breakfast. Cohn sat there beside the big pan of coffee, stirring it. It smelled of soup cubes. He said, "Not matter, not matter, missus."

Cohn's kitchen knife—Gerald is punished— A bucket of meat—The Als tunnel

The first soldier turned up for coffee at midday. I was still with Cohn, and I had no intention of going home. My mother had come out once or twice to call me, and so had my sister, but I did not in the least want to go back to the house and meet their angry glances, and have to see their reproachful faces. I was not feeling too friendly towards Gerald either, because the whole silly affair had been his fault, and I was sure that now he was making out to my mother and his that *I* had led him on to steal the pistol in the first place.

"Missus, mama calling," said Cohn. "You not going?"

I shook my head.

"Missus, missus, must do what mama say!" said Cohn. "Child must do what mama say!"

"Oh, be quiet!" I shouted. "*Must* do, *must* do, *must* do—yah!" I drove Cohn's big kitchen knife into the table so that it stuck quivering in the wood. "Must *not* do! Not! I'm going to do what I like, so there! See?"

"Yes, yes, missus," muttered Cohn, pulling his knife out of the table. "Not need to shout, missus, Cohn can hear missus all right!"

Even Cohn was no help today. I went out into the garden, where I ran into Gerald. His eyes were red from crying. "Your mama said my mama shouldn't hit me, but she did!" he said.

"Did it hurt?" I asked.

Gerald shook his head. "No, it didn't hurt, because she's not very good at hitting people, but I'm not standing for it all the same! I don't like her any more! I hate her! I'm going to run away!"

"Are you nuts?"

"No, I'm not. I'm going to run away. I've got a friend who lives in Alserstrasse and I'm going to stay with him. I often used to go to his place. He's got a *nice* mother!"

"And just how do you think you're going to do that? There are military police down at the crossroads. Do you think they're likely to say, 'Good morning, Gerald dear,' and let you through? They don't let anyone at all through, certainly not you."

"Then I'll go underground, so there!"

I said, "You're just stupid," and went away.

"I *am* going to run away and never come back—never, never, never!" Gerald shouted after me.

I spent all afternoon in the garden, near the fence between our house and Herr Wawra's. The Russians billeted in Herr Wawra's house were slaughtering a cow in the garden. I watched them skin the carcass and cut it up. They had a great many buckets, full of blood and meat and liver and lungs. One of the Russians waved to me. He had blood all over his hands, and his shirt and even his face were spattered with blood too. I crawled through the hole in the fence into Herr Wawra's garden, and he gave me a bucket of meat. Another Russian put a piece of liver on top of it.

The bucket was too heavy for me to carry, and I had to haul it along behind me. I was delighted. With a bucket of meat, I could venture to show my face at home again. No one was going to be cross with me if I brought them a bucket of meat.

I was right: no one was cross any more. Frau von Braun called me "darling," my mother smiled indulgently, and even my sister was nice to me. My father jokingly gave me the title of "Lord High Steward," but I knew that my father would have been nice to me even without my bucket of meat.

It was evening before we realised that Gerald was missing. He did not come in to supper, nor did he turn up later. Frau von Braun began to cry, and Hildegard said her prayers. My father searched the garden with the help of the Major's orderly.

I told them about Gerald's friend who lived in Alserstrasse, and how he said he was going there. Frau von Braun went down to the patrol at the crossroads, along with the Major. The soldiers there said no, they had not seen a fair-haired little boy, so Gerald had not been that way, and anyway he could not have got through the roadblock. It was pitch dark by now, and the Major decided it was no use searching any more; they would have to wait till morning.

"But where can he be?" my mother asked. "He can't just have disappeared off the face of the earth!"

Suddenly I remembered what Gerald had said to me. "I'll go underground, so there!" Underground? Underground! I knew which way Gerald had gone! Along the Als. There was very little water in the bed of the stream at this time of year, barely ten centimetres of water at the deepest spot. Gerald must have followed the stream to the mouth of the big concrete pipe where the Als went underground, to flow on through Neuwaldegg and Dornbach, under the Alszeile, through Hernals, beneath the Alserstrasse and all the way across Vienna until it reached the Danube Canal. Gerald and I had talked about this once, and I remembered telling him just for fun, "The Als gets wider and wider underground, you know, because of other streams running into it, and in the end it's enormously wide. If you look down through the gratings of the manhole covers in Alserstrasse you can see it gleaming down below and hear it rushing along!"

Moreover, I had boasted to him, untruly, that I had often climbed down through one of the manholes and went down a ladder into the Als tunnel, where there was a wide pavement beside the broad, gleaming river.

"You mean people can go for walks there, right underneath Vienna?" Gerald had asked.

"Of course they can," I told him. "Why, I once went to visit my friend along the tunnel. I climbed down into it near our building, and when I came home I climbed back up the same way. It was great!"

Oh, for goodness' sake, why did the stupid boy have to go and believe me? He was probably in the tunnel somewhere now. There were rats there too. I'd seen them through the bomb craters in the Alszeile. One thing was certain: he'd never be able to get up out of the tunnel through a manhole. The manhole covers were far too heavy. Gerald would need to be at least three times as strong as he was to lift one of those.

"It's late, child," said my mother. "Time to go to bed."

"And why don't you wash up for a change!" my sister snapped. "You stink!"

I would dearly have loved to go to bed. I would even rather have washed than told them where Gerald was. They'd be bound to say it was all my fault and be angry with me, and say I'd muddled up poor little Gerald with my tall stories.

Perhaps I was wrong, though! Perhaps he was not down in the Als tunnel after all.

The only person I could tell was my father, I decided. I would have to tell him when there was no one else about.

My mother was washing the dishes, with my sister standing beside her, having a wash herself. My father was sitting on the big bed, rolling a cigarette.

Perhaps my sister would need to go to the lavatory again. She was afraid to go to the lavatory by herself at night, and my mother had to go with her, taking a candle to light the way, and stand on guard outside the lavatory door. The dishes were washed. My sister was washed. No, she did not want to go to the lavatory; she got into bed. But then she got out again. She did want to go after all. My mother picked up the candle standing on the table. We had plenty of candles now; Ludmilla, the fat policewoman, had given my mother a whole box full.

"Come on, then," said my mother. She opened the door of the room shielding the candle flame with her hand, and went out, with my sister after her. I jumped out of bed. The first thing I did was close the door. My father had finished his cigarette, and was already in his nightclothes, which consisted of an old, pale green pullover found in one of old Frau von Braun's Biedermeier cupboards.

My father was attending to his legs, as he always did last thing at night. He had a wad of cotton wool—a very small wad of cotton wool; he had to go carefully with it, for who knew if the Major would give him any more when the present supply was gone?

"Are they any better?" I asked.

"Oh, so-so," murmured my father. "Don't really know." He pointed to a couple of the swellings. "The shell splinters have worked their way out here and there, but I haven't got enough bandages, or any disinfectant . . . they keep getting dust and dirt in them. You're supposed to keep something like this sterile, but there's always dirt about."

I slipped back to bed. Always dirt about! There'd be even more dirt in the tunnel. Too much dirt for my father's poor legs. The concrete tunnel through which the Als flowed was about a metre and a half high at its broadest, and my father was a metre ninety-five tall. He would have to crawl through the tunnel on his bad legs.

I must have sighed.

"What's the matter?" asked my father.

"Nothing!" I said.

"Worried about Gerald? He'll be back! I expect he ran off into the woods. But the weather's warm—he'll be all right!" My father tried to make a joke of it. "Unless a pack of wolves or a bear comes along!"

I shook my head. "No. He isn't in the woods."

My father put down the wad of cotton wool and looked at me with interest. "Oh. Do you know where he is?"

"Me? No, I don't know anything!"

"Now don't be silly. If you know anything, then tell me. Do you understand? You must tell me."

"But I don't know anything about it. How could I know anything about it?"

My father picked up his wad of cotton wool again and went on dabbing at the pus. "Don't get so excited," he said. "I only meant *if* . . ."

My mother and sister came back from their trip to the lavatory. "What is it? What's the matter with you two?" inquired my sister, who always had a nose for an awkward situation. "What's up?"

"Nothing!" I snarled.

"Oh, yes, there is! You look so funny!"

"I don't look funny! *You* look silly!"

"Stop it!" shouted my mother. "Stop quarrelling, the pair of you, calm down and go to sleep."

My mother licked her thumb and forefinger and pinched the wick of the candle she had been carrying. It hissed, and the flame went out.

"Have you washed?" my mother asked from somewhere near me.

I pulled the blanket up over my face.

"Of course she hasn't," snapped my sister. "What would she have washed in? There isn't any water in the basin, and she didn't go and get any while we were going to the lavatory, and the soap's quite dry!" (We had had a real cake of soap for the last two days. Ludmilla, the policewoman, had given it to my mother. It had a rather nasty rose perfume, and was violet-coloured.)

I stayed under the blanket, waiting for all the familiar noises: the creak of my sister's bed, the hiss when the flame of the big candle on the table went out, the way the big bed squealed as my mother settled in it.

All was quiet now, and I took the blanket off my face. It was pitch dark, with no moon or stars outside the window. I listened. Was everyone asleep? No, one of the usual night-time noises was missing; there was someone still awake. Was it my father? I sat up in bed.

"Daddy?" I whispered. And then again: "Daddy?"

"Ssh! Be quiet," said my mother.

I lay down again, trying to imagine myself rescuing Gerald from the Als tunnel. Going along beside the Als with a lantern. Calling "Gerald, Gerald" and going on and on. The tunnel got very wide, the Als became a huge lake. My lantern threw glittering light on the shiny black water. Cries of "Gerald—Gerald—Gerald" came echoing and reechoing back from the tunnel walls. There were rats swimming in the shiny black water, but I was very brave. I waved my lantern at them, making terrifying shadows flit over the water, and the rats were frightened and dived under. I went on. The tunnel got even broader, and there was more and more water, water coming towards me from all sides, a foaming, raging torrent. I was not afraid. I went on and on through the shiny black water with my lantern. I had tall gumboots on, and thick asbestos gloves with gauntlets up to my armpits. I found Gerald at the far side of the lake. He was whimpering and crying. I picked him up and carried him back. . . .

But I had no rubber boots. I had no asbestos gloves with gauntlets up to the armpits. I didn't even have a lantern. I wrapped the blanket tightly round my body and fell asleep.

It was very early in the morning, in the grey twilight, when my father woke me. "Want to come?" he asked in a whisper. "I'm going to look for Gerald."

I got up and dressed. I was freezing.

"Keep quiet," whispered my father.

The others were still asleep. I could not find my jacket, so I put my father's green pullover, the one he wore at night, over my flowered-quilt dress. We crept out of the room.

"Just the two of us?" I asked.

My father nodded.

"What's the time?"

"A little after four," said my father.

Outside the front door my father lit a cigarette. "Where are we going to look, then?" he asked me, in a tone of voice that seemed to show he was sure I knew.

"In the Als tunnel," I replied.

"An excellent idea," said my father.

I took his hand, and we crossed the meadow towards the stream. The grass was wet, and I had no stockings on. I got dew-drops on my legs.

"We'll need a lantern," I said.

"Gerald didn't have a lantern," said my father.

"But it's pitch dark in the tunnel!"

"You're an expert on the tunnel, are you?" asked my father.

"No."

"Ever been down there?"

"No."

"Well, then, keep your mouth shut!" muttered my father.

We were walking along the bed of the stream.

"It's a good thing it hasn't rained for so long," said my father, "or we'd have to swim!"

The Als was only about as broad as a fair-sized tree trunk, and ten centimetres deep at most. My father walked on one side of the stream, and I walked on the other. My father said, "After the first couple of metres it isn't all that dark in the tunnel. There are gratings in the manhole covers, and enough light to see by comes in through them."

"But . . ." I said. "But further on, under Neuwaldegger Strasse, it must be terribly dark. There's only a grating every third house there."

We had already passed the Archangel's house, and the next house after that, and we were somewhere behind the NSV Home.

"It doesn't matter whether it's dark or not under Neuwaldegger Strasse," said my father. "You can't get that far. There's an iron grille right across the tunnel under Atariastrasse."

"Why?"

"To keep out leaves and dirt, for one thing, and for another, so people can't get any further along. Otherwise anyone could just go wandering along the tunnel whenever they liked."

"How do you know?"

My father laughed. "I used to play around here a lot when I was a boy. We often walked out here from Hernals; I always wanted to go along that tunnel. I thought it would be terribly exciting to go all the way home along it and come up right by our building. Silly, eh?"

There was no need for us to crawl into the concrete pipe which was the mouth of the Als tunnel. Gerald was lying outside it, near a large clump of stinging nettles. He was curled up, with his knees under his chin, his arms clasped around his legs, and his head resting on a bundle tied up in a cloth. It was the fringed tablecloth from the Leinfellner villa's dining room; I recognised it at once. The bundle was an odd shape. I pushed at it with the toe of my shoe, and it clinked. A small jar of liver sausage rolled over the pebbles and fell into the water. I retrieved it.

Gerald stirred, and was instantly wide awake. He stared at me. My father laughed, and Gerald did look funny. His face was very dirty, a sort of greyish brown, with white rings left round his eyes, and the tip of his nose was pink. Evidently he was very cold; his teeth were chattering.

My father took off his jacket and put it round Gerald's shoulders. He looked at the bundle done up in the fringed table-cloth, shook his head, and asked Gerald, "Heavens, boy, couldn't you find yourself a softer pillow than those jars?"

Gerald looked hostile, because my father had laughed, and muttered, "I'm not stupid! I had to sleep on them because of the rats, so they wouldn't come and steal my food." He got up. There was a flat, pale brown object where he had been lying.

It was one of Cohn's maize-flour loaves.

"Pity!" said Gerald, picking up the squashed loaf. He turned to my father. "Will it still be all right to eat?"

My father shook his head.

Gerald sighed.

"Never mind," said my father. "We've found you, that's the main thing!"

"But I'm not going back," stated Gerald. He took the jacket off his shoulders. "I'm going on through the tunnel now. I'm going to live with my friend."

"Gerald, you can't get along the tunnel," I said. "There's a grille down there, under Atariastrasse, you couldn't get through."

My father nodded. "No one can go along the tunnel," he said.

Gerald looked at me. "But you said . . ."

"I was only making it up," I interrupted him. "For a joke."

Gerald stared at me. "Call that a joke? That's a rotten sort of joke. You've—you've . . ." Gerald looked as if he wanted to attack me physically, "you've told me a wicked lie!"

My father held on to Gerald. Gerald yelled, "She told a lie! She said you could go along the tunnel. It was *her* idea. She said she'd often been along . . . she's a nasty, silly pig!"

Gerald began to weep with rage, because he wanted to get at me and hit me, and he couldn't. My father was holding him tight. Gerald went on shouting, "She made me go down in all that dirt! It was smelly and horrible, and there were rustling noises. And it was all dark and scary." He pointed to the concrete mouth of the tunnel with the hand my father was not holding. "There were some sort of creatures in there, and it's all wet, and there wasn't any pavement, and I believed her, and I thought I'd find the pavement in the morning!"

"I never made you go down!" I shouted back. "I never made you go down there!"

"You told me a lie, though!"

I swallowed once or twice. "Yes, all right then," I said, "so I told you a lie! Told you a lie, a lie, a lie, a lie! Satisfied?"

Gerald was satisfied. My father was able to let go of him. He picked up Gerald's jacket and the bundle containing the jars of liver sausage. "Well, let's be off," he said. "The return of the prodigal."

However, Gerald was still unwilling to go home.

"Why not?" asked my father.

Gerald scuffed at the pebbles with the toe of his shoe, muttering, "It's so silly . . . it looks so silly!" He kicked out, and little stones shot up in the air. "You can't go back home again when you've run away!"

"Of course you can." My father kicked the pebbles too. "In fact, you must. They're all waiting for you."

"And they'll all stare at me in such a silly way," Gerald grumbled.

"They won't stare. They definitely will not stare," my father said soothingly.

"Promise?"

"Promise!"

They did stare, of course; they stared a lot. The first person to meet us was Cohn, who gave a shout of joy when he saw Gerald. I think he also gave thanks to some madonna of somewhere or other, but what with all the excitement he gave her thanks in his own language, and I couldn't understand what he was saying. Cohn's shout brought the others out into the garden. They were already dressed, and were probably about to set off in search of Gerald themselves. Frau von Braun ran to her son and hugged and kissed him, and pretty soon she was as dirty as Gerald himself.

The Major came out too, seized Gerald from Frau von Braun, picked him up, put him on his shoulders, and danced round in a circle. Gerald held tight to the Major's hair, and the Major began to sing, a loud and cheerful song. Cohn sang too. The Major's orderly came out of the house and joined in. The Major squatted down, with Gerald still perched on his shoulders, and began to dance the *krakoviak*: elbows outstretched, hands clasped under his chin, he leapt in his squatting position from one leg to the other, holding the leg on which he was not hopping straight out in front of him. It was spectacular. I was thrilled, and felt very envious of Gerald. No one had put on a performance like this for *me*!

Finally the Major was so exhausted that he tumbled over and fell in the grass, and Gerald toppled off his shoulders and rolled away.

"Come on, Gerald," said Frau von Braun. "I must clean you up!"

"I need something to eat first," said Gerald, rolling on over the meadow towards the house.

I needed some food too, but I was not keen on being present while they all made a fuss of Gerald and washed him and fed him attentively. I went off to the kitchen in the summerhouse. Cohn's coffee was ready, and I dipped a tin mug into the big pot, filled it, added sweetened condensed milk to my coffee and stirred. Then I sat down on the doorstep with the tin mug of coffee.

Memories: of Grandfather—Of Grandmother—
Of the crack—The horse—My idea—
The stories I told Cohn

So the days passed, one by one, all of them sunny, all of them different from ordinary, everyday life. Sometimes we had soap, sometimes we had none. Sometimes the Russians got drunk and shouted, sometimes they were wreathed in smiles. Every day we had beans and noodles with onions. Very occasionally we got venison. Sometimes Gerald would steal a jar of liver sausage from the cellar and share it with me.

The Major was handsome as ever. The sergeant got drunk. Ludmilla, who always had a hole in the toe of her stocking, had made friends with my mother. My father repaired watches and drank with Ivan. No one thought it odd that he could speak Russian any more, for by now everyone could speak a bit of Russian or a bit of German. Our little world extended from the roadblock in Atariastrasse to the roadblock in Hohenstrasse, a world consisting of one square kilometre. Suddenly I found that this was not enough for me. I wanted more. Indeed, I *needed* more; I found I was thinking about Grandfather more all the time. And Grandmother too. I loved Grandfather. (I suppose I loved Grandmother too, but I was not so sure about that.) If someone you love is dead, that is bearable, but you must at least know whether that person is dead or alive. I tried asking about Grandfather. I asked my mother, I asked my father, I asked Frau von Braun. They all said, "Yes, dear, of course Grandfather is still alive!" They said it just the same way they said, "Yes, dear, of course there is a Christ-child!"

I stopped asking them. I had noticed that my mother believed in the Christ-child, while my father did not. And Frau von Braun did not really mind one way or the other whether my grandfather was still alive.

That only left Cohn—Cohn with whom I could discuss anything, Cohn who did mind about things. He would know. Cohn knew where there had been fighting in the city, where buildings had been burnt down, where there had been a lot of shooting. Cohn cheered me up by saying, "Where Grandfather live not bad fights, missus, not bad fire, not many killed." He cheered me a good deal less by saying, "Maybe they very hungry, missus, not have food at all. Much people not have food, very hungry!"

I told Cohn a lot of things about Grandfather and Grandmother, since he was the only person who wanted to listen. Cohn particularly liked the sound of Grandmother, and would always say, "Good woman, good woman!"

I told him how fierce and angry Grandmother could be; indeed, I piled it on rather thick. But Cohn would not be moved from his conviction that Grandmother was "good woman." I kept wanting to talk about Grandfather, but Cohn always wanted to hear more about Grandmother. He even liked the sound of her eternal potato dishes, and he was not at all upset to hear that Grandmother would never let poor Grandfather have warm water for his footbath. "All good woman like that!" he said.

"You'd feel different if she looked at *you* so fiercely," I said.

Cohn smiled, and said he was used to that kind of a look. His mother had been just the same, and none the less she was "very good woman, could not be better."

Cohn was worried about the crack in Grandmother's ceiling. "Oh, missus, missus!" Cohn said. "Can be crack in walls a hundred years, and walls not fall down. But crack must not be bigger than so!" Cohn held up three fingers. "Or house all fall down."

How big *was* the crack in the ceiling? I seemed to remember it as at least five fingers wide.

The summerhouse-kitchen backed right onto the Archangel's garden now. There used to be a space of meadow about a metre wide between the back wall of the summerhouse and the fence, but that was before the Russians came, and now the fence was broken down here too.

The cart in which Cohn had arrived stood half in the Archangel's garden and half in ours. The horse that pulled it was stabled down at the local H.Q. with the other horses.

One day, when I had gone to see Cohn's horse with him, and as he was combing its mane while I tickled its nose, he said, "Poor horse! Poor thing, not go out for weeks. Not good for horse. Horse should run. Not right for horse to stand in room here!"

When Cohn talked about the "poor horse" and how it was "not right for horse to stand in room here," I suddenly had an idea. Cohn could take me into the city in his cart to see Grandfather. Cohn *must* take me!

When I told Cohn what he was going to do, he laughed and said, "Good, missus, very good! I drive, horse go trot, trot, trot!" And he clicked his tongue.

However, when he realised I was serious, he stopped laughing; he even stopped grooming his horse. "Oh, missus, missus!" he said. "Must be clever! Such a thing not good. Not possible!" He jabbed his forefinger into my chest. "You not can!" Then he jabbed it into his own. "I not can!"

"Why can't you?" I realised that *I* would not be allowed to.

"Because Cohn only very, very small soldier." With his dirty thumb and forefinger he indicated a distance of about a centimetre. "Small soldier like that, not allowed do anything. Only allowed obey orders. Only allowed do what is told. Not possible!"

"Well, why do you put up with it? Why not do what you like?"

Cohn shook his head.

"You're a coward!" I said.

Cohn smiled. His top tooth, grey and crooked, parted his lips right in the middle.

"That's what you are, just a coward!"

Cohn asked, "What is *coward*? Not know that word. What is *coward*?"

"A coward is . . . is . . . ." What exactly was a coward? It was difficult. "A coward," I began again, "is someone who's not brave, who's afraid!" Cohn looked at me, still baffled. "A coward is a person who is not a hero!" I said.

Now Cohn understood, and nodded, pleased. "Good, good, missus!" he said. "Cohn is coward, is great coward!" He pushed his lower lip up over his top teeth, and put his head to one side, so that it was almost on his shoulder. "I know many hero, I know many dead hero," he said. "Cohn still alive!"

I was not giving up. Every morning, and again in the middle of the day, in the evening, and at various other times in between, I would ask Cohn to take me to see Grandfather. I told him my very best stories about Grandmother, just the way I knew he would like to hear them. In my stories Grandmother grew taller and broader and fiercer daily. She picked up Frau Brenner because Frau Brenner said "Heil Hitler!" and put her in the big dustbin in the yard. She sang wonderful songs in a deep voice, and once she even danced on the kitchen table. I also made her cook delicious fritters. And I said that after she had been particularly fierce, she would always smile sweetly later on. At this point Cohn would whisper, "Like my mama, just like!"

Cohn wanted to hear that my Grandmother had a lot of children and even more grandchildren. One son and two granddaughters were nothing! So I humoured him, and endowed Grandmother with seven children and thirty-six grandchildren.

"Thirty-six?" Cohn wanted to make sure he had it right. "Ten and ten and ten and six?"

I realised I had been overdoing it. "Twenty," I said. Cohn was content with that.

The sergeant—Two shots—My sister's struggle— The siege

Then there came a day which seemed at first to be a bad day, but later I decided it was a lucky one. On this day I was woken by shouting, which made me feel anxious. Shouting and yelling in the morning boded no good.

The sergeant was shouting, and Ivan the military policeman was shouting too, and Ludmilla was also screeching something from time to time. No doubt the sergeant had been drinking all night again, and he had picked a quarrel with Ivan, and Ludmilla was trying to keep the peace.

I got out of bed, and found that my sister's bed was empty; she was in the big bed, in between my mother and father, being cuddled and having soothing remarks whispered to her because of the shouting Russians.

The window was open, and I sat down on the sill. Down below was the square terrace, and the room from which the shouting came had a door leading onto the terrace. It was Ivan and Ludmilla's room. I leaned out just as the terrace door opened, and Ludmilla came out. She looked very funny. Usually her hair was in a big bun on the nape of her neck, but now it was loose and hung down to her hips. Ludmilla's only garment was a silk nightie the colour of a pink pig. Her mountainous breasts and even more mountainous behind wobbled under the pink silk. She was hopping from one bare foot to the other; the stones of the terrace must have been cold. She was looking back into the room through the terrace door.

Then Ivan came out on the terrace. Much to my delight, he was completely naked, with nothing on at all. To my even greater delight, Ivan, stark naked, was pushing the sergeant in front of him. The sergeant was both dressed and drunk, too drunk to stand, and Ivan was holding him by the collar. Ivan kicked his bottom. The sergeant fell over. Ivan pulled him up again by his collar, the sergeant stood there swaying, and Ivan kicked him once more. The sergeant took a stumbling step forward, and fell over again. Ivan pulled him up, kicked him, let him fall, pulled him up again.

In this way Ivan kicked the sergeant right across the terrace, giving him a particularly hearty kick when they reached the four stone steps leading down to the garden. The sergeant toppled down the steps and lay there in the ivy. Ludmilla shouted something angry at him, shaking her fist, which made her breasts wobble alarmingly. Ivan spat in the direction of the sergeant, and then he and Ludmilla both went back to their room. I heard them close the terrace door and turn the key in the lock.

My family, in the big bed, asked me what was going on, and I told them. They came over to the window to have a look at the sergeant lying there in the ivy.

"Has he broken his neck? Is he dead?" asked my sister.

"No, unfortunately not," murmured my mother, for the sergeant was just beginning to move. He tried to get to his feet, and found it beyond him. He crawled through the ivy on all fours until he came to the end of it, where there was a small stone bench. Holding on to this bench, the sergeant hauled himself up, lay facedown on the bench for a moment, then heaved himself over and sat down.

"He'll go to sleep now," said my father, but he was wrong. The sergeant did not drop off to sleep. Instead, he stood up.

"Is all that row going to begin again?" asked my mother crossly. "Can't the brute give us some peace?"

"He's going away!" said my sister, relieved.

The sergeant was making his unsteady way along the gravel path. He collided with the pear tree, embraced the pear tree, let go of the pear tree, and suddenly we saw that he was holding his pistol. His new pistol. The old one, the one we had put in the garden gnome's wheelbarrow, was hidden under my father's mattress; he had retrieved it from the meadow.

Pistol in hand, the sergeant pushed off from the pear tree and staggered on.

"Keep away from the window!" said my mother.

"He could never hit us here!" said my father.

I stayed by the window. I wanted to watch the sergeant reel out of the garden gate. However, he was not making for the gate. Where *was* he going?

Oh, no! No, he couldn't! It wasn't fair! Cohn had not done anything to hurt him. Why did he want Cohn? Why was he getting closer and closer to the summerhouse?

I grabbed my father's arm. "Is he going to get Cohn?" I asked.

My father nodded. "Just like him—the cowardly swine!"

The sergeant was standing outside the summerhouse door, kicking it and shouting. The door was thin, with an oval pane of glass in the top half. The sergeant kicked the door in, making a big hole, but not big enough for him to get through. He fired his pistol twice, aiming at the lock of the door. The door opened, and the sergeant disappeared into the summerhouse.

"I can't bear it. I can't watch," said my mother. She left the window and sat down at the table. I followed her and sat beside her. Even there, in the middle of the room, we could still hear the sergeant shouting.

There was not a squeak to be heard from Cohn.

Then a shot rang out. And another. My mother put her hands over her ears.

"One of them went out of the window," said my father.

"What about the other?" I asked. I was surprised to find I could speak at all.

My father did not know where the second shot had gone. The sergeant had stopped shouting now, and the garden was perfectly quiet. My mother took her hands away from her ears. "What's going on now?"

"Nothing moving," said my father.

"Nothing at all?"

"Nothing at all."

I began to cry. I couldn't help it.

"Hush," said my mother. "You won't get hurt. The sergeant won't come in here."

"Cohn," I sobbed, "Cohn!" I couldn't utter anything more, just "Cohn . . . Cohn."

My mother looked at me hard. She had put her thumb to her mouth, and was nibbling the nail. Then she rose from the table and went to the door of our room. "Cowardly swine," she said, not to me or my father or my sister, but to herself. "Cowardly swine, the whole lot of them! Pretending not to hear! Scared silly! I suppose our fine heroic Major has been struck deaf all of a sudden!"

"What are you going to do?" cried my father. "Don't be a fool! You can't go down there. That idiot will shoot you. Don't be so crazy!"

My mother was opening the door, and she did not look as if she were frightened. I wasn't frightened for her either; I just wanted her to do something to help Cohn.

"If he's shot him, there's nothing you can do now," said my father. "And there must still be two shots left!"

But my mother was already out of the room.

My father tried to follow her, but my sister hung on to him, clinging and screeching, "No, don't leave me alone! Stay here! Don't go!"

She was holding my father's pullover tightly with one hand and clinging to her bed with the other, but my father still tried to get out of the room, dragging my sister, bed and all, along behind her. Then her bed got wedged between the big bed and the table.

"Oh, for God's sake! Let go!" said my father.

My sister let go of the bed and clawed at his pullover with her other hand too. I was surprised to see how far an old green pullover will stretch. My sister's strength surprised me too. But I couldn't spare any time watching her, because I was standing in the doorway of the next room, which opened near the head of the stairs. I wanted to see what my mother was doing.

As it turned out, my mother had no heroic notions of marching off to the summerhouse to confront the sergeant and rescue Cohn. She had simply gone down to the ground floor, where she was rousing the Major and his orderly and the red-haired soldier; she knocked on Ivan's door too. And she kept calling them all names. She called them a lot of names in German, and a number of others in Russian, and she even called them some names in Czech which she had learned from the Czech woman who used to be caretaker of our building in the Geblergasse.

The gist of what she was saying, translated and somewhat abbreviated, was something like this: "Come on out then, you heroes, you splendid victors, you cowardly lot! What do you think you're doing, pretending to be asleep, you rats? Are you so scared of one drunken sergeant? You should be ashamed of yourselves! Lying low like this! Hiding from an idiot who's firing his pistol off around the place! Couldn't care less what's happened to that poor cook, could you? Yellow! Lily-livered, the lot of you! If that cook bleeds to death it's your fault, and I'll tell you so to your faces! Go on, then, leave him to die, why don't you, you rats?"

The more my mother shouted the louder she got, and by now she was positively bellowing. She shouted herself hoarse.

I ran downstairs and stood in the corner of the hall, by the cellar steps.

My mother was still shouting, getting hoarser all the time. Very slowly, the Russians emerged from their rooms. First the Major's orderly with a self-conscious smile on his face. My mother glared at him. Then Ivan and Ludmilla came out, and then the others. The last to appear was the Major. None of them was angry with my mother, in spite of all the names she had called them and the way she had shouted. They seemed rather ashamed to face her, and I realised it was because she had made them feel ashamed that they were now prepared to go off to the summerhouse. Perhaps they were a bit ashamed to face each other, too. One thing is certain, they would never have lifted a finger for Cohn of their own accord.

The Major spoke to the others, explaining something and waving his arms about, giving orders and generally acting as if he were preparing for a tremendous battle. Then they all got out their pistols, and they left the house with the Major in the lead, and the others behind him, all keeping close together.

I ran to the middle window of the salon, which had a good view of the garden and the summerhouse.

The Russians were just coming round the corner of the house. The Major gestured to the others, and walked slowly along the gravel path to the end of the lilac bushes. Here he stationed himself behind the pear tree which the sergeant had been embracing not long before. The others stayed by the corner of the house.

Turning to the summerhouse-kitchen, the Major shouted something like, "Come out, come out at once, you dog! And drop your gun!" Inside the summerhouse nothing moved.

The Major ducked; keeping low, he popped out from behind the pear tree, scuttled over to the Japanese fir, and shouted again. He was a metre closer to the summerhouse now, but he was still ten metres off. The others crept over to the lilac bushes from the corner of the house and lay in wait there, pistols cocked.

Still nothing moved in the summerhouse-kitchen.

I felt that this could go on for ever, with the Major darting from tree to tree like that. And how was he going to cover the last four metres, where there were no trees, only a snowdrop bed?

I left the window, walked through the salon, through the hall and out of the house. No one saw me; no one was bothering about me. The men outside were staring at the summerhouse, and everyone else inside was staring at the men outside who were staring at the summerhouse.

I ran across the meadow to the bed of the stream, went along it, splashing through the water, and reached the Archangel's garden. I crawled through the currant bushes, over the trodden-down fence where the Angel always used to walk with her doll's pram, crawled along on all fours until I reached Cohn's cart, and then wriggled my way under the cart to reach the back wall of the summerhouse, which had a little window in it. I wanted to get cautiously to my feet and look in through the window . . . and yet I didn't want to. I was afraid of seeing Cohn lying dead inside.

I stood up—and jumped! I heard Cohn's voice, not from the summerhouse window, but right behind me. "Missus—pssst! Here! That you, missus?"

Cohn was in his cart, crouching there in his grey long johns. Gooseflesh showed through the silky hair on his chest. He whispered, "Came out through window, when idiot there kicked door in!"

I climbed up beside Cohn in the cart. "Are you cold?" I asked.

"Not matter, not matter, missus." Cohn smiled. "Not see you," he told me, "only see bright patch."

He did not have his glasses on.

"Glasses inside, on bed," he explained.

The Major's voice floated over to us, across the broken fence, the currant bushes and the summerhouse roof. He was trying to lure the sergeant out. He must be three metres closer to the summerhouse-kitchen by now.

"Do you think the sergeant will shoot?" I asked Cohn.

Cohn wagged his head thoughtfully. "Not know. Not can tell."

Stew everywhere—The sergeant is moved out—
Cohn's glasses—A family quarrel—My idea again—
A sore throat—The rubble

The sergeant did not shoot. I heard Ivan give an all-clear signal. Ivan had decided the Major's method was taking too long, and went charging right through the snowdrop bed, with the safety catch off his pistol. When he reached the summerhouse and looked in through the open door, he began to laugh and was quite unable to stop. He beckoned to the others.

I climbed down from the cart and hoisted myself up to the window at the back of the summerhouse. It really was a funny sight! The sergeant was lying on the red and white paved floor, fast asleep, covered all over with noodles and rounds of sliced carrot and cabbage leaves and beans. His uniform was sodden with greasy liquid. Cohn's big pot, the one he used for making soup and stew, lay on its side next to the sleeping sergeant, and Cohn's big wooden spoon rested on the sergeant's stomach.

The Major's orderly came into the summerhouse and took the sergeant by one arm, while Ivan took him by one leg. Between them, they dragged him out. I saw his head bumping on the stone floor as his nose ploughed through the stew. His forehead knocked against the doorstep.

Ivan laughed; so did the Major's orderly. They dragged the sergeant a bit further. His head was facedown on the gravel and sand and dust and little bits of grit stuck to the grease on it. There was some blood too. They took the sergeant off to their local H.Q. under arrest.

"What a pity you couldn't see it!" I told Cohn afterwards.

"Is not pity, what I not see," replied Cohn.

I tried to describe the sergeant all covered in stew.

Cohn shook his head. "Was not so much vegetable in stew like you say was on Serge."

Serge was the sergeant's name.

"You're not *sorry* for him, are you?" I asked.

Cohn did not know if he was sorry for the sergeant or not, but he wanted me to find his glasses.

I went and looked for them. They were not on his bed; they were under the table. One side of the frame was bent, and the lens in it was cracked. There were three little cracks and a small hole in the glass where they met. Either the sergeant or Ivan must have stepped on Cohn's glasses.

For once Cohn did not say, "Not matter, not matter, missus." He tried to straighten out the frame, and in doing so broke it. Accusingly, almost weeping, Cohn held the glasses out to me.

"Not matter, not matter," I said.

"Does matter, does very much matter!" said Cohn, upset. "Glass broken, frame broken, can't see!"

However, he managed somehow, by sticking the broken side of the frame to his cheek with sticking-plaster. Like that he could wear his glasses, but he went about all morning complaining bitterly and holding one hand over the broken lens.

"What are you doing that for?" I asked. "Your eye doesn't hurt!"

"What you say, not hurt! Of course not hurt! But with eye open I not see. Not see through other half either."

I wanted to talk to Cohn that afternoon, but somehow I couldn't manage to get a real conversation going. He was avoiding me. I asked him at least ten times, "You'll need a new pair of glasses now, Cohn, won't you?" Cohn just grunted noncommittally.

That afternoon he washed his socks and his shirt. I was baffled. Cohn had never washed his socks and shirt before. I pointed out the washing line in the summerhouse window and the wet laundry on it to everyone, but no one else was interested.

That evening I found Cohn bent over his uniform jacket in the summerhouse, attacking it with a brush and some strong-smelling ammonia.

I sat down beside him.

"Hullo, missus, hullo," he said. But he did not tell me why he had washed his socks and was now cleaning up his jacket.

I went to bed feeling furious, muttering crossly to myself. "Calls himself a friend! Cross with me just because his glasses get broken! Oh, shit!"

My father said Cohn was not really cross with me.

"But he won't tell me why he's washing his socks!"

"Well, what business is it of yours if he's washing his socks?" asked my mother.

"It *is* my business, it damn well is! Everything is!"

"Oh, of course," said my sister sarcastically. "Naturally, *everything* is her business!"

I threw the copy of *The Easter Hare's School* at her head, and she howled that I'd broken her nose.

"Your goddam nose isn't broken!"

My mother lost her temper, and said I was to stop using such vulgar expressions at once, this minute, or I should grow up speaking no better than a common drayman. A very common drayman.

"But everybody says damn and shit!" I shouted back. And I went on yelling, "Shit, shit, shit!" till my mother boxed my ears. Then I plumped up my pillow, cried a little, although she had not really hit me nearly hard enough to hurt, just brushed the side of my head, wrapped my blanket round myself, and closed my eyes.

I was pleased to hear my father standing up for me, telling my mother that everyone in the house really did say "shit," even my mother herself when the stove was smoking or the sergeant shouting. "Well, what about it?" said my mother. "She'll just have to break herself of the habit. Things will eventually get back to normal, and she can't go back to school talking like that."

"Oh, she'll drop it soon enough then," my father said soothingly. I vowed to myself that I never would, and I'd never go back to school again either, and I was going to do all I could to make sure things never did go back to normal. I decided I liked things better when they were not normal.

When I woke up and was lying with my eyes closed, sorting out the various morning noises, I heard several unfamiliar sounds. As well as the twitter of the blackbirds, and Ludmilla's high-pitched voice, and Gerald's attempts to whistle, I heard a sound of snorting and trampling. I ran to the window—and then I knew why Cohn had been washing his socks and brushing his jacket.

Cohn was walking up the gravel path, shaved, washed, combed, his glasses stuck on with a fresh piece of plaster, and he was leading his horse past the summerhouse towards the cart.

Cohn was going out!

I threw my flowered-quilt dress on, putting on my sister's knickers by mistake in my hurry. The knickers, being too big for me, hung revoltingly loose between my legs.

Cohn was just putting the horse into the shafts when I reached him.

"Where are you going, Cohn?" I asked.

"Going into city," said Cohn, sighing. He took a note out of his uniform pocket. It had something written on it in foreign letters.

"Must go to hospital," he said, tapping his note. "In hospital I get new glasses, for be able to see again."

The slyness of it! Now I realised why he had been so unwilling to talk to me yesterday. He had known perfectly well he was going to drive into Vienna today, and of course he knew equally well that I would be desperately eager to go with him. He was already shaking his head, although I hadn't said a word yet, and saying apprehensively, "Missus, missus, no good, no good, won't, can't, not possible!"

"But Grandmother!" I cried. "My grandmother, Cohn! You like my grandmother so much! I've got to go and see my grandmother!"

"I go and see Grandmother," Cohn whispered. "Your papa write me down the way."

He took another piece of paper out of his trouser pocket. There was a sketch map of Hernals on it: the Hauptstrasse and Kalvarienberggasse and a red dot to mark where our building stood.

Cohn pointed to the back of the cart, where some old blankets were lying. "Underneath is bag for Grandmother, your mama fill it. Things for Grandmother to eat, if Grandmother still there. But of course Grandmother still there!"

Cohn was giving the horse a carrot.

"I want to go too!" I said.

Cohn shook his head firmly. "No one go too, can't take no one too!" And then, to comfort me: "I come back this evening, bring news from Grandmother and Grandfather, bring new glasses!"

The horse had finished the carrot, and Cohn went into the house. He needed Ivan to put yet another rubber stamp on the piece of paper with the foreign letters.

When Cohn was out of sight I climbed up into the back of the cart, lifted the blankets off the bag of food and looked inside. There were packets of noodles, a bottle of oil, beans, and two jars of liver sausage. I lay down beside the bag and covered myself with the blankets. I waited. The blankets were scratchy and dusty, and smelled of dog. They gave me a tickle in my nose.

I heard gravel crunch on the path, and held my breath, thinking it was Cohn coming back, but it was only Gerald. He came up to the cart, shouting a rude rhyme in the direction of the Angel's garden, lifted the blankets and asked me, "What are you doing there?"

Up to this point I had not been quite sure what I *was* doing.

Really I was only waiting for Cohn to come back, find me, and turn me out of the cart. But now I said, "Go away, cover me up, I don't want Cohn to see me!"

Gerald climbed onto the cart and tucked the blankets round me. "Here he comes," he suddenly whispered, and I heard him jump down.

Cohn came closer. The cart gave a jerk, moved backwards, Cohn called, "Gee-up" and clicked his tongue, the cart rumbled and shook, and something hard in the bag bumped against my head. It felt as though Cohn were driving with two wheels in the soft earth of the tulip bed and two on the gravel path. Then he got all four wheels on the gravel. He called, "Whoa!" and the cart stopped.

I heard Gerald shout, "I'll open the big gate for you."

The big gate squealed. I pushed the blankets off my nose so that I could breathe more easily.

Cohn was turning into the road. The cart was not jolting now, and I knew when we reached the local Russian H.Q. because the soldier on duty at the roadblock called out something to Cohn and laughed, and Cohn laughed too, and shouted something back.

I did not want to stay underneath the stifling blankets much longer. I enlarged my airhole till it was a peephole. We had already reached the tramline terminus. I decided to stay under the blankets till we got to the Hauptstrasse in Hernals. Once we were that far, surely Cohn wouldn't turn round and take me back.

It took ages. I seemed to remember the way as being much shorter. But at last I saw green branches overhead, belonging to the trees lining the Hernalser Hauptstrasse. I put my head out from under the mound of blankets. Hesitantly, I said, "Cohn!" and then again: "Cohn!" Cohn did not hear. He was sitting at the front of the cart, singing softly to himself. I crawled out. Cohn turned around and stared at me.

I tried to produce an innocent smile. "I went to sleep in the back of the cart, Cohn, and when I woke up again you'd driven off." I made my way to the front of the cart and joined Cohn on the driver's seat. "Let me have a go!" I tried to take the reins.

"No, missus, no!" said Cohn crossly. "You make trouble— much, much trouble. What I do with you now? Tell!"

"Well, you can take me to see Grandfather and Grandmother. And then in the evening, when you've got your new glasses, you can come and fetch me."

"Suppose Grandmother not there?"

"Oh, she's sure to be there." I looked at the ruined buildings all along the street. "She can't have gone out shopping, and Grandfather can't be out at work either."

"But suppose not there at all? Not any more?"

"Oh, Cohn," I said, taking his sleeve and holding it very tight, "Cohn, you kept saying you were sure they weren't dead. You promised me—you did promise!"

Cohn frowned and shrugged his shoulders. "Did promise? Did not promise!" And then: "Not possible to promise people alive. Did *want* they be alive, understand, did *want* it." After a while he added, "Well, missus, we soon see." He said no more, and I did not feel like discussing it myself.

Twice Cohn was stopped by a patrol of military police, and had to show his pass, with Ivan's rubber stamp. Each time he pointed to his broken glasses, and then to me, and explained something to the soldiers. First the soldiers laughed about the broken lens, and then they stroked my hair. "What are you all saying about me?" I asked.

Cohn looked at me resentfully. "Missus, I must tell lie for you! Must say you are very sick child, much sore throat and stomach pains, must go to hospital too."

"Oh!" I said, grinning.

"No 'oh!,' missus! You not laugh, is nothing funny! Papa and mama at home worry, worry much about missus, look for silly missus everywhere!"

Cohn took my father's sketch out of his trouser pocket, and pointed to the line with "Kalvarienberggasse" written beside it. "Missus, where that? You show me where I leave big street?"

Yes, indeed, where was it? Everything looked very different from the old days. I was not quite sure just where we actually were. We had been under the railway viaduct. Perhaps we had reached Wattgasse? There'd always been a furnishing store at the corner of Wattgasse and the Hauptstrasse with red signs above the shop windows, red signs with yellow lettering. And next door there was a shop with a blue pole from which a white swan hung. But I could not see any red signboard or any white swan, nothing but a great mound of rubble.

The undamaged Mayor—A hole as big as a bathtub
—The heavy thing on my feet—The piano—
The doll's house

"Well, missus? Where is?"

Everywhere, as far as I could see, there were vast piles of rubble, with ruins standing among them, and here and there an isolated undamaged building. Then I saw the church, so I knew we were heading in the right direction. "Keep going, just keep going," I said.

Cohn drove on. The going was difficult in places because there were bomb craters in the street, and Cohn's horse did not like passing bomb craters. Each time Cohn had to get down, stroke the horse, and lead him round.

We came to Elterleinplatz. I knew where we were because of the island in the middle of the square, with three lilac bushes and a statue of a mayor. The island and the Mayor were still undamaged. Nothing else within sight was undamaged—nothing else at all.

"You have to turn left somewhere here," I said.

Cohn nodded. However, turning left was impossible. There was nothing to our left but a gigantic yellowish-brown pile of rubble, and a lot of dust glinting in the sun. Even at a distance the dust tickled our noses, made our eyes sting, and stuck to our gums.

A man was crawling around on the heap of rubble, looking for whole bricks and making a stack of them. When he saw us, he ran off so fast that he dropped a good brick which he had just been wiping clean.

"Hi, hi!" called Cohn. "Not run, you stay, talk!"

But the man took no notice of us.

"Hi, hi!" Cohn waved his sketch map, and jumped down from the cart.

"Never mind him, the fool!" I said. "I know my way!"

Cohn did not listen to me. He jumped onto a heap of rubble and ran after the man, sinking in knee-deep. Thick yellow dust swirled up.

"Cohn, come back!"

In my anxiety to fetch Cohn back, I jumped out of the cart and clambered up on the mountain of rubble myself. It was a steep uphill climb for about five metres, and I had to go carefully.

I found myself standing on a kitchen dresser, a white-painted kitchen dresser, with one foot on the drawer for cutlery and the other on the drawer for bread. There was a cracking sound underneath the kitchen dresser, and suddenly I saw a hole open up in front of me and the dresser—a hole the size of a bathtub, only much, much deeper. And broken bricks, bits of wood, stones, and mortar were slipping and falling and tumbling into the hole from all sides. I stood there staring at the hole, watching it gradually fill up, feeling the kitchen dresser itself begin to slip under my feet, and I jumped back, onto one end of a big wooden beam. The other end of the beam, which was buried in the rubble, shot up out of the debris with a loud noise. My end sank deeper and deeper into the rubble.

"Cohn!" I shouted.

I was sitting on the beam, up to my chest in rubble now. My arms were free, and I was trying to shovel the debris away with my hands, working at it madly, but no sooner did I clear a little away than a new lot would slide down to fill in the space. I was getting tired. I stopped yelling for Cohn. Suddenly a huge fall of rubble came sliding down: broken bricks, bits of wood and glass, stones, a piece of plaster the size of a plate—bright blue with a pink rose on it. It smelled horrible: of cellars and bombs and war. But the war was over! There was not a single plane to be seen or heard in the blue sky overhead.

The pink rose on the bright blue background hit my head. Pieces of plaster scratched my face. The sky was still blue.

"Missus! Where are you, missus?" Cohn's voice sounded hoarse and desperate, and a long, long way off. The stuff on top of me had stopped hurting; things still came raining down over me, but they felt as soft as cotton wool. Everything was all right.

The only odd thing was the absence of any plane with a string of silvery beads hanging down from it. I closed my eyes.

When Cohn hauled me out of the rubble I screamed because there was something lying across my legs, something heavy which hurt. I wanted Cohn to leave me where I was, and then the heavy, painful thing would not hurt any more. Cohn would not leave me where I was.

He'll pull my legs off, I thought. My legs will get left behind here in the rubble. However, they did not get left behind. Cohn pulled me free and dragged me down from the rubble, scolding me. I hung over his shoulder. Sometimes my feet were dangling in the air, sometimes they knocked against beams and walls. Cohn's glasses were sagging forward from his cheek, only now both lenses were cracked. His uniform, cleaned with ammonia only last night, was covered with dust.

Cohn put me down on the cart, where I lay on my back looking up at the sky. The bomb ruins among the heaps of rubble were going round me in circles, round and round, faster and faster, rushing by, falling in on top of me.

"Where hurt, missus?"

It did not hurt anywhere.

Cohn could not believe it. He tested every joint in my body.

"That hurt?" he asked, bending my legs at the knee, tapping my ribs, pulling my fingers, patting my throat.

"You're tickling me," I said.

Cohn sighed, wiped the dirt from his forehead, muttered, "Missus, missus, very lucky, oh, very much lucky!"

I sat up. My head hurt, but the bomb ruins were standing still. "Now you're all dirty again," I said.

"Not matter, not matter, missus," said Cohn, slapping his trouser legs. Dust swirled out of them. Then he pushed the broken glasses up the bridge of his nose.

"Can you see anything?" I asked.

"Not see," said Cohn.

"Are you sure?"

"Ah, well," muttered Cohn, "will be all right."

We drove on along the street, and turned left. "Is here?" asked Cohn. No, it was not here.

"Missus, look there!" cried Cohn. "Look. What word for that?"

"Piano!" I said.

Up above us, among the beams and broken roof and shattered window frames of a bombed-out building, there was a black piano hanging upside down, keys underneath and pedals on top.

"Piano," Cohn repeated. "Very beautiful piano!"

I was relieved. So Cohn could see something after all. We turned another corner, and there stood the ruin of our own building, still looking like a doll's house with the front off it.

"We're there," I said. Cohn nodded and stopped the horse. Cohn got down from the cart and took out the bag of food. "Come on, missus!" he said. "Come on."

The locked door—The wrong Grandmother— Grey socks—A nasty meal

We went towards the doll's house ruin. The windows of Grandmother's room were boarded up, which was a good sign; dead people don't go nailing boards over their windows.

The door of Grandmother's room was firmly closed too, but a narrow, well-trodden path led up to it.

Cohn grinned in relief.

I ran along this path, the last part of which led through Grandmother's old kitchen. One of the pale blue-tiled kitchen walls was still standing, the gas stove in front of it. The gas lighter and striped pot holder still hung from the pale blue tiles. The door into the room was locked.

"She's not at home after all," I said, discouraged. My grandparents never used to keep the door of their apartment locked.

Cohn knocked on the door, and there was a rustling sound behind it. He knocked again. I helped him.

"Who's there?" It was Grandfather's voice.

"It's me!" I shouted, rattling the door handle.

"Juli said she saw a Russian soldier coming," said Grandfather, fiddling with the lock on the inside of the door.

"That's Cohn," I explained through the keyhole. "He brought me."

At last Grandfather had the door open. It took a long time, because the door stuck, and the door stuck because the walls of the building had settled.

I hugged Grandfather, and Grandfather asked a whole lot of questions all at once. Where were the others? How are they? How did I come to be here on my own—and a great many other things. I said everyone was very well, and held tight to Grandfather, feeling the tufts of hair in his ears tickle my cheeks.

Cohn stood by the door, grinning, wagging his head and staring into the dark room.

I let go of Grandfather. "Where's Grandmother?" I asked.

Grandfather pointed into the room behind him. "Back in there somewhere. She's afraid of that soldier." He pointed at Cohn.

Grandmother, afraid! That was new. Grandmother never used to be afraid of anything. I went into the room, and Grandmother came to meet me. She looked quite different from the way I remembered her. She was much smaller and much thinner, and her hands shook. She stroked my face with her shaking hands, pressed me to her bosom and sobbed, murmuring, "To think of seeing you again, to think I should live to see the day!"

I was feeling very uncomfortable about all this, especially on Cohn's account. I had told him stories of an entirely different Grandmother. A tall, stout, fierce Grandmother. While this Grandmother was small and rather thin, and not at all fierce.

"Why are you crying?" I asked.

"To think I should live to see the day—just to think of it!" sobbed Grandmother, reaching out for me again with her shaking hands.

"Her nerves have given way," said Grandfather.

"Must go now," said Cohn. "Must go for glasses." He bowed to Grandfather. "Will come back with glasses, fetch missus!"

Grandfather bowed to Cohn. Grandmother stood there trembling, not understanding what was going on.

Cohn turned, went through the half-kitchen and along the narrow path.

"He's going!" said Grandmother, relieved. She stopped shaking quite so much. "Russian swine!" she added.

I ran after Cohn and caught up with him where the door of

the building used to be. "Cohn, please hurry, come back for me soon!"

"Yes, missus, yes," murmured Cohn. "Will hurry, yes."

He stopped, looking at me through the smeared lens of the glasses tied to his head. "That was Grandmother?"

I looked at the heaps of rubble. I wished I could have said: No, Grandmother is dead, Grandmother is buried under the rubble. And it would not have been so much of a lie either. My own grandmother really had gone. Of course, she had never really been as big and fierce and magnificent a figure as I had described to Cohn, but neither had she been so small and trembling and pitiful as the old lady back there in the doll's house kitchen.

"Not matter, not matter," said Cohn. "I fetch missus quick, very quick."

But Cohn did not fetch me quick.

I sat in Grandmother's room all day. Grandmother would ask me a question, I would tell Grandfather the answer, and he would shout it into Grandmother's ear—the left ear—because she was stone deaf in the right one.

It was dark in the room, and very little light came through the boards over the windows. Grandmother had a laundry basket full of socks, all of them dark grey with two green stripes at the tip—German army socks from the Wehrmacht camp on the Gürtel. Grandfather had brought them home one day.

Grandmother sat by one of the windows, which had a crack between the boards so that a little light came through, cutting the green stripes off the tops of the socks and trying to catch the stitches of the cut edges again. She was not doing the job very well, because her hands shook.

"What's she doing that for?" I asked Grandfather.

"So that no one will see they're German army socks."

"Why shouldn't they?"

"They could tell that they're stolen."

Stolen? If you took army socks from a camp belonging to an army that no longer existed, was that stealing?

"But whose would they be now, then?" I asked.

Grandfather did not know.

"Oh, Lepold," complained Grandmother, "Herr Brenner brought paraffin home, and Herr Simon got some lard, and the others got flour and things, and Lepold brings home socks, nothing but socks! He's no good for anything."

"You silly cow," said Grandfather.

"What?" asked Grandmother, offering him her left ear.

"You silly cow," said Grandfather.

"What was that?" asked Grandmother.

"It's nearly eight o'clock!" Grandfather cried into her left ear.

"I hear you," said Grandmother. She put a sock into the laundry basket and got supper. She took an old tin can out of the cupboard and put it on the table. Three holes had been bored near the top of it, each the size of a small coin. Grandmother stuck some small, thin splinters of wood through the holes, and put a pan on top of the tin.

"Nice soup!" she said to me. "Light it!" she told Grandfather.

Grandfather took a box of matches from his pocket. "Our last," he said. He struck a match on the side of the box, shielding the flame with one hand, and put it to the holes in the tin. The match went out before the splinters of wood could catch fire.

"Oh, he thinks he can do everything better," snapped Grandmother. "I shake so much, I'm not allowed to! He can always do everything best!"

I always kept a box of matches in the pocket of my flowered-quilt dress, and I happened to have two there at the moment. I gave them to Grandfather, who promptly pocketed them.

"I want one! Give me one!" cried Grandmother. "Give me one at once!"

Grandfather was not parting with the boxes of matches.

Grandmother seized my hand. "One of them's mine! Tell him one belongs to me!"

I didn't know what to do. Grandparents quarrelling over matchboxes was something outside my experience.

I realised that tears were streaming down my cheeks. I was not quite sure why I was crying. The only thing I *was* sure of was that I wished Cohn would come.

But Cohn did not come.

Grandfather lit the little bits of wood stuck in the tin, and Grandmother stirred the pan. It smelled nasty.

When the soup was ready Grandmother handed it to me on the forget-me-not plate, my favourite plate. The wooden-handled spoon was still there too. I put the spoon in my mouth, empty, and it tasted just the way it used to, a rough, bitter taste of iron and salt.

"Don't you want anything to eat?" asked Grandfather.

I shook my head. Grandfather pulled my plate towards him.

Grandmother shot him a venomous look. "Always him, always him," she muttered.

By now it was dark outside, as well as in the room. I went into the doll's kitchen with Grandfather, and we sat on the floor.

It was pitch dark, and still Cohn did not come.

I could hear Russian voices in the distance. Cohn? No, not Cohn. Two voices. Military police, no doubt.

The voices came closer, passed the piles of rubble. One voice was laughing, one was talking.

Grandfather put his hand over my mouth; I was not sure why.

The voices faded. The voices were gone. Grandfather removed his hand again.

"The Russians don't do a lot of bad things," I said.

Grandfather nodded.

"Only about the same as other people. . . . Most of them are very nice."

Grandfather nodded.

"I like them. Specially Cohn."

Grandfather nodded a third time.

"Anyway, why shouldn't they hear us?"

"Because I'm afraid," said Grandfather.

Afraid! Afraid! Everyone was afraid.

"You'll have to sleep the night with us," said Grandfather. "That soldier isn't coming back."

" 'That soldier!' " I was furious. "Don't say 'that soldier' like that! He's Cohn. He's my friend, my best friend!"

"Don't get so upset," murmured Grandfather.

We looked at the sky for a while, but there was nothing to be seen, no moon or stars or clouds.

"Sometimes planes fly over," said Grandfather.

"Over us too," I said.

"Some of them are American planes," said Grandfather.

"Not the ones that fly over us," I said.

"How do you know?" asked Grandfather.

"I just do," I said.

"Perhaps we'll be lucky," said Grandfather. "Perhaps the Russians will go away and the Americans will come."

"I don't want the Americans!"

Grandfather was silent.

I realised that Cohn was not coming back today. It was absolutely dark, there were no street lights anywhere, and not one of the few undamaged windows showed a light, so Cohn would never be able to find his way.

Grandfather got up, and so did I. He lit a match, and we groped our way through the doll's house kitchen. The match went out at the door of Grandmother's room, and Grandfather lit another.

The match threw flickering shadows on the double bed where Grandmother slept, lying on her side with her mouth open. She looked terrible, because she had taken out her false teeth, as she did every night.

"Please, will you leave your teeth in?" I asked Grandfather.

We took off our shoes and sat down on the bed. The match had gone out.

"Do you want to sleep on her side or mine?" asked Grandfather.

I really wanted to be in the middle, but I could not do that, because there were only two blankets, so I crept into bed with Grandfather.

Soon Grandfather was asleep too. It was very quiet; neither of them snored or snuffled. The only sound was an occasional rustling outside the door of the room, or a creak in the ceiling overhead. I remembered about the crack in the ceiling. What had happened to that crack? I had not thought about it all day, and it was so dark in the room all the time that I had not seen it.

Perhaps Cohn would come for me after all. I had kept my dress on, just in case. I liked to sleep on my front, but the buttons stuck into me, so I turned over on my back, bumping into Grandfather.

"Go to sleep," muttered Grandfather.

I went to sleep.

When I woke up it was light in the room; someone had opened the boarded-up windows, and I saw my father standing by one of the windows. He had his back to me, I was glad to see. I closed my eyes again.

"I had no idea you didn't know she was here," I heard Grandfather say.

"There was nothing you could have done about it."

"I'd have brought her home."

"What, past the police and through the roadblock?"

"Yes," said Grandfather. He really seemed to believe he could have done it.

My father came over to the bed—I could hear his footsteps on the squeaking floorboards—and tapped me on the shoulder. "Get up," he said.

I did not move.

"You're not asleep," said my father, tapping harder. "Your eyelids are quivering!"

I tried rolling my eyes upwards behind my closed lids. Gerald said that if you rolled your eyes up as if you were trying to look at your brain, your lids wouldn't quiver. Gerald's trick did not work. My eyelids went on quivering.

My father said I should stop pretending, and Grandmother, who appeared to be still in bed beside me and still toothless, judging from the way she hissed when she spoke, wailed, "Oh, let the poor little thing have her sleep! Leave her alone for a bit; she's so tired."

"I've got to be going," shouted my father.

"What was that?" asked Grandmother.

"He's got to go!" shouted Grandfather.

"Oh," said Grandmother. "Oh."

All this shouting, I realised, would have woken even some-one as deaf as Grandmother. I sat up.

"Get dressed," said my father.

"I am dressed."

"Put your shoes on, then."

I got out of bed and bent down. My shoes were there, but I stayed on the floor as if I were searching for them.

"Hurry up, put your shoes on," said my father.

I put them on, and then said I had to wash, and do my hair, and I was hungry.

"Oh, come along!" said my father. "Say goodbye, and come on!"

My father took my hand and pulled me. I resisted. He let go of my hand, and I fell on the bed.

"You are the stupidest, most pig-headed child I've ever met," my father told me, leaning over me.

"Cohn's coming to fetch me," I said.

"Cohn is not coming to fetch you."

The way in which he said that convinced me it was true. I stood up and said goodbye.

Grandfather kissed my cheek; Grandmother pressed me to her trembling bosom. I pulled free. My father was pressed to her bosom as well, and then he too was free. We left the room, and Grandfather closed the boarded windows again.

We set off out of town, going along Geblergasse, walking fast. I took my father's hand. "Don't run like that!" I gasped. "I'm getting a stitch!"

My father stopped, took a cigarette out of his pocket, put it in his mouth and lit it. I wanted to sit down on the side of the pavement, but he said, "No, you can't," and pulled me up. I took his hand again and we went on. Some way further on, near the railway line, I wanted another rest. "I'm tired!" I sobbed.

"So am I," said my father. "Come on, now. You can sleep as long as you like once we get home. There's not much time left. We have half an hour at the most to reach the roadblock by the tramline terminus!"

Why did we only have half an hour at the most to reach the roadblock at the tramline terminus, I asked?

"Because the guard will be changing in half an hour's time."

What did that have to do with us?

"I've got a note from the Major saying they must let me through the roadblock."

So what was the matter, then?

"Listen, the Major's note isn't really worth the paper it's written on. He has no authority to let civilians through."

Then how had my father got through in the first place?

"Because there happened to be one drunk and one good-natured fool on duty at the roadblock!"

Well, then, that was all right, wasn't it?

"No," my father explained. "I can't count on the next couple of guards being drunk and good-natured too! And if they're not they won't let us pass, and we shall be stuck on this side!"

I was in a hurry now myself. I got no more stitches, and I did not feel tired either. I ran on, with my father running and limping and panting beside me.

"Are you cross?" I asked.

"No," said my father.

"What about Mummy?"

"Don't know. Anyway, she'll be glad to have you back safe!"

"How did you know where I was?"

"Gerald."

"Did he tell you straight away?"

"No, not till the evening."

"Why didn't Cohn come back for me?"

"He's locked up."

I stopped dead.

"Come on!" said my father.

I did not move. Cohn, locked up! "Because of me?" I asked. "Because of me? He can't be. He couldn't help it. He didn't know. We must tell the Major he didn't know!"

My father said it was not as simple as all that, and if I would be a good girl and keep running he'd tell me all about it, or all he knew, which was only as much as Ivan knew. Ivan had had a phone call about Cohn yesterday evening.

So as I ran on, my father told me, "We do know for certain that Cohn got his new glasses, and now he's under arrest, suspected of being a deserter."

"But he isn't a deserter!" I cried.

"Well," said my father, "we know he drove off from the hospital, and then his cart broke its axle, but instead of reporting it Cohn unharnessed the horse and went on with it."

"What, riding?" I asked.

My father did not know; all he knew was that apparently Cohn had lost his way and been picked up by a military patrol, and was now suspected of being a deserter.

"But he was coming to fetch me!" I said. "He was going to take me home. That's the only reason he left the cart. We must tell them!"

"That won't do him any good."

"But what *can* I do for Cohn?"

"Nothing."

"But it's my fault!"

"Don't talk such nonsense," said my father. "It may or may not be your fault—that has nothing to do with your ability to help. Do you see?"

"What will happen to him now?"

My father shrugged his shoulders.

"Will they shoot him dead?"

My father said no, they would not shoot him dead, because the war was over now and sentences were no longer so harsh.

"Will I see him again?"

My father thought I probably would not see Cohn again. I wouldn't be seeing much more of the others either, the Major and his orderly and the sergeant and Ludmilla and Ivan and all the rest, because they were all leaving in a few days' time.

"Is the war really over now? Are all the soldiers going away?"

No, all the soldiers were not going away. But the Russians we knew, who were front-line troops, were being relieved, and the Army of Occupation was coming instead. Occupation. I didn't like the word. I didn't want any Army of Occupation.

The inn—The good-natured man—Helpers for Papa —My mother has a struggle with herself

My father did not look forward to the arrival of the Army of Occupation either; he said no one liked the idea. But I did not get round to asking what the Army of Occupation would be like, because we were coming up to the roadblock at the next corner.

"You walk along right beside me now," said my father, "and if I give you a nudge then run—run as fast as you can, understand?"

"Where to?"

"Out of Neuwaldegger Strasse and round to the other roadblock, in Atariastrasse. Wait for me there. Ivan's on duty there today, and he knows all about it."

"When will you come?"

"As soon as I can. I don't know yet. Perhaps it will all go smoothly and I shan't need to nudge you, and you needn't run."

The military police patrol was stationed in a small inn near the spot where everyone had to stop. The inn had a green door and a window, and a sign with its name, *Zur lustigen Emmi,* above the door. Above the window hung another sign advertising Hauer wines. There were no curtains at the window any more, and no benches or tables left inside the inn, just the big brown bar, which was still there, and a camp bed with a grey blanket on it.

There were supposed to be two Russians on guard duty standing outside the door the whole time. The men on guard were watching out not only for civilians, but for other Russian soldiers, who were not allowed past the roadblock and into the city unless they had a pass stamped three times and signed twice. However, there was no one standing outside the inn door now.

We were about ten metres from the door.

"Let's both run, really fast," I suggested. "I don't want to go on my own."

"Suppose they're looking out of the window?" asked my father.

"Let's get down and crawl along the ground!"

"Oh, don't be silly," said my father. "This isn't a game of Red Indians!"

He stopped. It was very quiet. I looked at the tramlines, seeing the little blades of grass growing up between the paving stones and the metal rails. I looked at the manhole cover, and saw two red and black spotted beetles crawling across it, one on top of the other.

One soldier came out of the inn and looked at the blue sky. He had no gun, and he did not look drunk, so it must be the good-natured one. Recognising my father, he grinned and waved. My father grinned back. Then the good-natured soldier looked up at the sky again, pretending he didn't see us. We came level with him, and went past him. He was still looking at the sky.

The drunken soldier was sitting at the open window of the inn, leaning his head on the window sill, asleep . . . no, not asleep. We were three paces past the window when he bellowed behind us, *"Stoy!"*

My father gave me a nudge, and then another. I ran. I ran and ran, faster than I had ever run in my life. Neuwaldegger Strasse was long. Neuwaldegger Strasse was never going to end. Neuwaldegger Strasse couldn't possibly be this long!

A fence of palings, wooden railings, metal railings, wire netting, wall, wooden railings, metal railings, wall . . . asphalt, earth, cobblestones, earth, asphalt . . . jasmine, lilac bushes, silver firs, box tree, jasmine, silver firs, box tree . . . Number 20, enamel number-plate, Number 28, metal number-plate, Number 36, Number 44 . . . wall, paving stones, silver firs, Number 52, enamel name-plate saying Atariastrasse, Ivan at the door of the house! Ivan laughing, Ivan stretching out his arms, Ivan calling, "Our girl back, our girl back!" Ivan picking me up, tossing me up in the air, catching me again, rocking me like a baby.

I struggled, and Ivan let go of me, putting me down on the seat outside the house the Russians were using as their local H.Q. in this area. I told him what had happened down at the other roadblock—how the good-natured man had looked at the sky, but the drunk had woken up.

"Then what?" Ivan rubbed his big nose with his thumb and forefinger. Some other soldiers had come out of the house, looking curious. "Then what?"

"Then I ran, fast!" I said.

Ivan thought this was hilariously funny. The others thought it hilariously funny too. They roared with laughter. Ivan asked me three more times, "Then what?" and I had to answer three more times, "Then I ran, fast!" And each time the soldiers and Ivan laughed.

Further up the road, in the Archangel's house, there was a lot of noise. A crowd of Russians singing. There were Russians singing in the other houses too, Russians singing everywhere. I had been too agitated to notice before. Even the sergeant, our much-decorated sergeant, who was still under arrest because of the shooting incident in the summerhouse, was standing at the window of the lock-up singing. He kept singing something that sounded like, *"Vetscherni svon, vetscherni svon. . . ."*

My soldiers kept on laughing.

I felt both desperate and furious. "You're all drunk!" I cried.

They laughed and nodded happily.

"You're stinking *drunk!*" I yelled.

They laughed and nodded again, and Ivan scooped me up once more. "Not be angry, sweetheart!" he murmured. "Not be angry!" Holding me against his chest with one hand, he pointed with the other to the Archangel's house, to the house behind him, the Leinfellners' villa, all the places where Russians were billeted. "Not be angry, all big party, party for goodbye. All go away, much away, far away, much goodbye!"

Oh, for God's sake! I thought. Singing happily away as if everything were all right, as if my father wasn't down at the other roadblock with a drunken Russian policeman.

I beat at Ivan's head with my fist as hard as I could. It hardly seemed to bother him; he went on singing, and so did the other soldiers.

"Go and help Daddy, can't you?" I yelled in his ear. Even Grandmother could have heard that. Ivan went on singing.

I went on beating at his head with my fist and shouting, "Ivan, help him, for goodness sake!" Finally my yells seemed to make their way through his befuddled ears and penetrate his befuddled brain.

He stopped singing. "Help who?" he asked.

"My daddy!"

"Who?"

"Daddy!"

Ivan stood still. I slid out of his arms, over his chest and down to the ground. Ivan looked at me, bewildered.

Oh, what was the matter with him? Why did he keep asking such silly questions, why didn't he *do* something?

"What is *Dad-dy?*" asked Ivan.

Dear heavens above! What is daddy? I yelled, "Daddy, papa —daddy is papa! You must help Papa!"

Ivan beamed happily. He got the idea. "Help papa!" he laughed. *"Da, da,* help papa!" Suddenly he was all eagerness to help Papa. So were the other soldiers. Indeed, they all insisted on going to help Papa, and no one wanted to stay on duty at H.Q. Finally they found a young soldier who had a poor head for drink, and was leaning against the wall of the house next door, asleep on his feet and snoring, his head hanging and his arms dangling, with his cap on the ground in front of him. They woke him up, talked to him, shook him, and told him he was standing guard. He staggered, looked blearily up at them, his face a greyish green, ducked his head down between his shoulders, blinked at the sun, drew his head even further down, and went into the guardroom.

Ivan shouted something after him. He turned and picked up his gun, which he had left leaning against the wall.

Among Papa's would-be helpers was a man who had the keys to the patrol car. He said *"Nyet"* at first, but then he handed them over. The patrol car was an open vehicle like a jeep. Ivan got behind the wheel, and the other soldiers climbed in, with me wedged between them. Apart from Ivan, there were at least eight of them.

We drove down Neuwaldegger Strasse, driving sometimes on the right-hand side of the road and sometimes on the left—not that it mattered, since there was no other traffic about. We would narrowly miss first a wall on the left, then a tree on the right.

The soldiers were enjoying themselves. But down at the bend in the road, near the tramline terminus, Ivan did something wrong. The car went slower, stopped, gave a jerk, stopped again, gave another jerk, and stood quite still.

Ivan tried and tried to start it, muttering, "Shit!" to himself.

However, since swearing at the car did no good, we all got out of it, leaving it where it was in the middle of the road, and continued on foot, with Ivan and me in front and the other soldiers behind us. They were all shouting in chorus, "Help papa, help papa!"

The good-natured man was standing at the door of the inn, smoking a cigarette, and the drunken one was sitting at the table waving his hands about. Beside him stood the two men who had come to relieve the guard, and obviously neither of them was drunk. One was holding a piece of paper, and the other had my father by the arm. My father was talking in a mixture of Russian and German and then more Russian, talking about the Major, pointing to the paper with his free hand and repeating "Major" every few seconds.

Papa's helpers, with Ivan still at their head, came into the room. I stayed outside, watching through the window.

Ivan was standing between the two new guards and my father, who had both arms free now, because the new guard was holding Ivan's arm instead and showing him the piece of paper, explaining to Ivan how the Major's note was not worth anything, and it was none of the Major's business, and the whole thing was against regulations.

Ivan looked at the paper, studying it with interest. The other soldiers crowded round him. They all wanted to see the paper too. They stretched out their hands for the paper. The new guard refused to let go of it. Ivan insisted. In fact, he had no real authority in the matter at all, but in some way it seemed that Ivan ranked higher in the army than the new guard, and so eventually the man let Ivan take the paper after all. Ivan crumpled it up in a little ball and put it in his pocket, explaining that as it really was *not* worth anything he didn't want to see any more of it. The drunken soldier protested, the new guard protested, and so did his companion. Papa's helpers surrounded them all, asking each other vaguely what was going on, and pushing my father further and further away from the guards in the process, until he was right outside the whole confused crowd of Russians. They manoeuvred him over to the door and made signs to him to run.

But the good-natured guard was still standing at the doorway with a gun. My father looked at him, and hesitated. He dared not risk walking out past him. The back row of his helpers were getting impatient, gesturing and jerking their heads at the door.

The good-natured guard was staring at the ceiling of the room, examining the pale blue glass lampshade with pink lilies on it. My father ran. I jumped down from the window sill and followed him, quite surprised to find how fast a person with shell splinters in his legs can run if he has to. Somewhere around Number 30, past the bend in the road, we stopped running, because the inn was out of sight, and my father said we would attract less attention if we walked. We walked slowly; my father was limping and panting and sweating. It was midday by now, and the sun was blazing down. There was no one on the street.

My father wiped his forehead. "That turned out all right after all!" he said. "The stupid fool wanted to have me sent off to the central Russian headquarters back in the city!"

"What would they have done to you?" I asked.

"Oh, if they were in a good mood they'd have sent me home next day. If not, I suppose they'd have sent me to Siberia!" My father laughed. "Well, *now* I feel sure they'd have been in a good mood, but a few moments ago, back there"—he pointed behind him—"I wasn't so sure!"

The man on duty at the local H.Q. did not seem to think much of his job. As we passed Atariastrasse we saw him leaning against the wall of the house in the sun, asleep again. We did not disturb him.

The singing in the Archangel's house had stopped, and there was only one voice still to be heard in the Leinfellners' villa further up the road. All was quiet in the other houses too.

"They're tired," said my father.

"It's only midday," I said.

"Well, they've been celebrating a long time. They started yesterday afternoon."

I asked if the Russians were really going away? My father explained again that it was only this lot of Russians who were going; other Russians would replace them, and it was always like that. First came the combat troops, then the Army of Occupation. What exactly was an Army of Occupation? Well, not combat troops. Why was an Army of Occupation worse?

"It's not that the Army of Occupation is worse," said my father, "but the combat troops are better. They're more important, so they get more to eat and more to drink, and they have more money and can do more. Do you understand?"

I understood.

"And people who have more things, and can do more," my father went on, "tend to be nicer to other people!"

I understood that too.

"These Russians gave us things to eat, because they had plenty for themselves. But the Army of Occupation won't have enough, and they'll want *us* to provide *them* with food."

"How do you know all this?" I asked.

"I spent long enough in Russia!"

"Did you get to know a lot of Russian soldiers there?"

"Russian soldiers, no!" My father laughed. It was not a happy laugh. "Plenty of German soldiers, though!" And he added, "There's no difference. None at all."

Perhaps he was right. Probably he was right. We had reached the fence of spears now, and were going in through the garden gate.

My mother came out of the kitchen, thanked God, and asked my father if it had been difficult. She did not look at me.

"Well, you've got your little chicken back again," said my father.

My mother looked at me now, crossly.

"Come on!" said my father, laughing. "Please, no sermons about the shocking way she's growing up. Be glad we're back all right, and let it go at that!"

My mother sighed as she asked if I was hungry. I was indeed hungry, ravenously hungry. I went into the kitchen, where she had new Russian bread and tinned butter and apricot jam. There was tea to drink as well.

My mother sat down beside me, and I could see her struggling with herself. She wanted to be cross, because mothers are supposed to be cross if their children run away, but then again, I was the only person here who could give her news of Grandmother and Grandfather and how they both were. If she scolded me and preached me a sermon she wasn't going to hear my news.

So I asked in nice, quiet, polite tones, like a good little girl, "Shall I tell you about Grandfather and Grandmother?"

My mother sighed and said, "Yes, please, tell me!"

I told her a lot and talked for a long time, and if I did not always stick exactly to the truth, it was only so that my mother would like my story and find it reassuring.

Boxes of clothes—The summerhouse again—
The bean pot—The message—
Things are ugly without people

"When do you have to leave?" I asked Ludmilla.

"When are you going away?" I asked the Major's orderly.

"How much longer are you staying?" I asked Ivan.

They did not know. Sometime. Tomorrow morning, or this evening, or the day after tomorrow, or perhaps not till next week.

I asked Frau von Braun; I was sure she would know more details, because she spent so much time with the Major. Every time Frau von Braun mentioned the Russians' impending departure her eyes filled with tears.

Gerald would mutter, "Silly goat!" and go out of the room.

Three days went by, and nothing happened. Ludmilla's cardboard cartons full of clothes and things were standing in the hall, all corded up, waiting to be fetched. Ivan had a last, final, farewell drink with my father seven times a day. The Major sat in the kitchen and sang something that sounded like *"cherniod-schikrasniodschi,"* and carved a little wooden doll with my father's best knife. The wooden doll was to have hair; the Major was bent on having some particular sort of hair for this doll, and we could not understand what he meant. All we grasped was that the Major was quite sure we must have some of this hair about the place. He searched the house, and eventually found what he wanted behind the iron door where the big water-pipes were. He was after hemp fibres, and he took them off the pipes, which were wrapped with sacking.

Frau von Braun was deeply moved by this gesture. My mother was not; she was afraid the pipes might leak. As for me, I was cross because the Major was carving the doll as a memento for Hildegard. "You can have it once he's gone," Hildegard said.

"I don't want it," I told her. And I didn't really want the doll, which was not a particularly nice one. The thing that annoyed me was that the Major was not going to all this trouble for *me*.

Old Herr Wawra was ill. He lay in his summerhouse, snuffling and coughing, with a rattle in his throat. My mother took him soup at midday, and Frau von Braun took him noodles in the evening, but he often did not touch the soup or the noodles.

The Archangel came round to ask where people were being buried these days, and whether funeral arrangements and so on were in working order again.

"Dying is always in working order," said my mother.

The Angel was filthy, in a much worse state than the rest of us, and really she was quite friendly now. However, we were traditional enemies, and enemies we would remain, no matter how friendly the Angel was.

Gerald told me about his latest plan. He was going to build a hut of leaves and branches in the woods. I promised to help him, but I never did. I spent most of my time sitting in the summerhouse. I did not expect Cohn to come back. I didn't even think of him much. I just liked sitting there, on Cohn's bed, wrapped in Cohn's blanket, looking through the open window and watching Gerald prancing about, watching Ludmilla wash her stockings, watching my sister whispering to Hildegard, listening to the Archangel's querulous voice, listening to the Major laughing and Ivan shouting. Sometimes I heard my mother calling for me. If anyone disturbed me in the summerhouse I felt annoyed. I decided to move in there entirely, but my mother did not think that was a good idea. For one thing, she'd have been against it anyway, and for another, as she explained, "It wouldn't be worth it now. We shan't be here much longer!"

I shouted that I would be very good at living alone, and I could cook myself much nicer things in Cohn's big pot than my mother gave me, and I'd sleep much better in Cohn's bed, too, because I wouldn't have to listen to my sister snoring and grinding her teeth. In the midst of this tirade I suddenly realised what my mother had said. It wouldn't be worth it because we shouldn't be here much longer. . . . What did she mean? What nonsense! What absolute nonsense! "I'm going to stay here for ever and ever!" I said.

"Oh. Going to buy the villa from old Frau von Braun, are you?" asked my mother.

"No," I cried. "I can't buy anything because I haven't got any money, but she can't throw us out, she isn't here any more. It belongs to us now, and Gerald and Hildegard and young Frau von Braun too, of course!"

"A delightful idea!" said my mother.

"Old Frau von Braun will be coming back, don't you worry!" said my father.

"Suppose she's dead?" asked my sister.

"Then someone or other will inherit this villa." My father grinned. "But you can bet it won't be us!"

"If the Major and Ivan stand at the gate and say 'Nyet,' then the people who've inherited the villa won't be able to come in!"

"Talk about silly ideas!" my sister giggled.

I went to find Frau von Braun. She was in the kitchen with a big pot of water. There were brown beans at the bottom of the pot, and wrinkled beans floating on top.

I showed a suitable interest in the beans, fished one of the wrinkled ones out of the pot, squeezed its skin off, extracted the sprout and crumbled up the rest.

"Is old Frau von Braun still alive?" I asked, crumbling the bean.

"You can be sure she is," said young Frau von Braun. "That sort live to be over a hundred! Tough as old boots."

No one inheriting the place, then! "Will she come back and live here?"

Young Frau von Braun shrugged her shoulders.

"My mother said we'd soon be moving out." I waited: waited for an indignant denial, waited for Frau von Braun to say, "No such thing!" Or: "Oh, no, you must stay!" Or: "Out of the question!"

Frau von Braun nodded. "Yes, I know."

"I don't want to," I muttered.

"Don't want to what?"

"Go."

"You won't be going tomorrow," Frau von Braun reassured me. "You may not be going for some time yet." She looked at me, and then at the bean pot, staring into its depths as if there was something very fascinating to be found there. But whatever it might be, she did not find it. She looked at me again and said, "They're leaving tomorrow morning. I've only just heard."

"Oh, no!" I said. And then: "Perhaps they'll put it off again."

"Not this time, no, not this time," said Frau von Braun to the bean pot.

"Perhaps he'll come and see you sometimes."

Frau von Braun started, and stared at me. "Who'll come and see me?"

The silly goose! Who did she think I meant? Why was she looking at me like that?

"Who?" Her voice sounded shrill.

I could have said: The Major, of course! But I said, "Oh, no one!" and left the kitchen. I went to see Ivan.

"You'll be gone tomorrow," I said to Ivan.

Ivan nodded.

"Where are you going?" I asked Ludmilla.

"Tchermany. Bloody Tchermany," said Ludmilla.

I asked if they were going to have another farewell party that night. But they said no, they had celebrated their departure once already, and celebrating twice was not allowed. Besides, they had to be off at four in the morning.

"Not can get up with headache!" laughed Ivan.

I asked him whether he would be seeing Cohn again in Germany. Ivan thought it likely that Cohn would rejoin them once they got there.

"Then please will you give him my love?"

"What you say?" asked Ivan. My sentence had been beyond him; it was outside his vocabulary.

"Tell Cohn . . . tell Cohn . . ."

"What tell Cohn?"

Yes, what *did* I want him to tell Cohn? "Nothing," I said.

Ivan looked puzzled, asked again, "I tell Cohn nothing?"

I nodded. Ludmilla grinned.

That night I lay awake for a while thinking about the Army of Occupation and how I wished they would never come. In the middle of the night I woke up. I climbed out of bed, crept over to the door of the Uncles' Room, and knocked over something small as I did so. It fell with a clink, and my mother sat up in bed.

I froze. Could she see me? No, she couldn't. She lay down again, and the bed moaned. I waited till the bed stopped creaking, and my mother's breath was coming regularly. Why I went to the attic after that I don't quite know, but I opened one of the attic windows and looked out. I saw lights down in Atariastrasse, far more lights than were usual at night. There were three huge trucks standing there with their headlights on, illuminating the space in front of our local Russian H.Q. There were carts standing there, with horses already in their shafts. I realised that carts were standing ready all along our road too—outside our own fence, the Archangel's fence, Herr Wawra's fence, and the fence of the Leinfellners' villa.

I closed the attic window, went downstairs again, and crept into bed. There was a glimmer of light from the Uncles' Room. I must have been up in the attic quite a while, for it was already a little less dark outside.

I intended to get up at four to watch our Russians leave, but it was midday when I woke.

I went all over the house. I found one of Ivan's socks—a sock with a hole in it, its sole black and hard with dirt. I found a sheet of paper with writing in foreign letters, and a bit of braid with a button on it. A pink lace bra hung from one window, its elastic worn out and its metal fastener rusty. A bra with no Ludmilla, a Russian letter with no Major's orderly, a sock with no Ivan.

There were things lying round everywhere. I found a leather strap in the garden, and also a dinner plate, a vest lying near the fence, a bottle in the street, and a tin pail near the Archangel's place.

Things are ugly without people.

I went out of our garden and kicked the bottle. It rolled down the street, and I ran after it. I found that the roadblock at the crossroads was gone. The door of the local Russian H.Q. was open and an old man and a young woman were clearing things out of the house. Russian things. An armchair with only two legs, bottles and paper and rags and other such rubbish.

"Will the next lot of Russians have a base here too?" I asked.

"No!" said the old man. "No one else is coming here!" He told me there would never be so many Russians again, and the roadblocks were gone for good too. The government, he said, would be Austrian again, and Austrians wouldn't go blocking the streets against each other. The young woman and the old man loaded all the rubbish on a handcart and took it out into the garden at the back of the house to burn it.

Three days later the Army of Occupation arrived. The soldiers moved into the villas which were standing empty, not the houses where people were living. Their uniforms were more yellow and less grey, their red stars were bright and clean, and they never sang at all.

I kept expecting one or other of them to come to our house for our beans and noodles and the last of our jars of venison, but they didn't. My father often went off into the city, and when he came back he would tell us about empty apartments, and talk about two rooms and three rooms, and requisitions and permits and grants. One day he came back bringing a fat woman with him. The fat woman had a horse and cart. She drove into the garden, and helped my mother load boxes and bundles and pillows on the cart. I remembered how we had come here with just one bag.

I sat on the back of the cart, surrounded by blankets and cans of oil, leaning against a big blue bag of noodles. The noodles scrunched.

My mother got up beside the fat woman on the driver's seat. "Well, we're off," she said. "Take a last look!"

I closed my eyes.

About the Author

Christine Nöstlinger was born in Vienna in 1936. She has published eight novels for young readers. In 1972, she was awarded the Friedrich-Bödecker Prize for her contribution to children's literature, and in 1973, the German State Children's Book Prize. She is widely recognized in Europe as an outstanding talent in the field. Franklin Watts is her first publisher in the United States.

Date Due

10/13/76			
5/18/77			
3/8/78			
5/10/78			
5/11/78			
10/10/79			
12/1/79			
3/10/81			
11/6/83			
10-30-07			

BETH ISRAEL LIBRARY
VINELAND, N. J.